THE PHOENIX OF MADRID

Calderón de la Barca

THE PHOENIX OF MADRID

No hay burlas con el amor

Translated by Laurence Boswell

OBERON BOOKS
LONDON

First published in 2011 by Oberon Books Ltd
Electronic edition published in 2012

Oberon Books Ltd
521 Caledonian Road, London N7 9RH
Tel: 020 7607 3637 / Fax: 020 7607 3629
e-mail: info@oberonbooks.com
www.oberonbooks.com

A catalogue record for this book is available from the British
Library.

PB ISBN: 978-1-84943-134-7
E ISBN: 978-1-84943-694-6

Cover design by Rosemary Butcher

Visit www.oberonbooks.com to read more about all our books
and to buy them. You will also find features, author interviews and
news of any author events, and you can sign up for e-newsletters
so that you're always first to hear about our new releases.

Characters

DON ALONSO

MOSCATEL

DON JUAN

DON LUIS

DON DIEGO

LEONOR

INES

BEATRIZ

DON PEDRO

This translation of *The Phoenix of Madrid* was commissioned by Theatre Royal Bath, and was first performed in the Ustinov Studio, Theatre Royal Bath on 14th September 2011 with the following cast:

DON ALONSO Milo Twomey

MOSCATEL Peter Bramhill

DON JUAN Adam Jackson-Smith

DON LUIS Tom Mothersdale

DON DIEGO Christopher Hunter

LEONOR Laura Rees

INES Samantha Robinson

BEATRIZ Frances McNamee

DON PEDRO David Fielder

Director, Laurence Boswell

Designer, Ti Green

Lighting Designer, Ben Ormerod

Sound Designer, Fergus O'Hare

Movement Director, Lucy Cullingford

Fight Director, Gordon Kemp

ACT ONE

The house of Don Alonso de Luna.

Enter DON ALONSO and MOSCATEL.

ALONSO: What the hell is wrong with you?
You've been wandering about for days
Ignoring orders, talking nonsense
And to double your iniquity
You appear when I haven't called
Then when I call you run and hide:
What's the matter? Speak.

MOSCATEL: Oh, alas!
These sighs come up from my soul.

ALONSO: And is it right for a servant to sigh
In front of his master?

MOSCATEL: We rogues:
Do we not have souls?

ALONSO: Of course:
For feeling your rough hewn emotions
And complaining at enormous length;
But not for sighing, sighs are the sign
Of a noble passion.

MOSCATEL: And, sir:
The passion that fills my soul
Is a noble one.

ALONSO: Utter nonsense!

MOSCATEL: Is there a nobler passion than love?

ALONSO: You know, I rather think there is:
But to save us both a lot of time
I'll say, there is not.

MOSCATEL: There is not? Well:
As the passion I suffer is love,

          My passion is a noble one!

ALONSO: You! Love?

MOSCATEL: Me love!

ALONSO: If that's the cause
          Of this nonsense, I will laugh
          More heartily at today's pinning
          Than at yesterday's rapture.

MOSCATEL: Because you have never known
          What it feels like to be in love:
          Because you have always chosen
          The wild ways of the libertine:
          Because the only pleasure you
          Enjoy in love's sweet name,
          Is to break a young ladies heart
          And laugh at a young man's dreams:
          Because you've tricked so many
          Without giving your heart to one:
          Because you play the game of love
          Like a cunning card sharp who's
          Hiding all the aces up his sleeve:
          You think it's funny to mock me
          A man who is truly in love.

ALONSO: I won't employ a lovesick servant!
          Go and find yourself a new master.

MOSCATEL: But think!

ALONSO: There's nothing to think about!

MOSCATEL: Listen!

ALONSO: What would you like to say?

MOSCATEL: In the theatre there is always
          A lovestruck nobleman with his
          Servant standing by fancy-free.
          Is it my fault that fortune's
          Turned everything upside down?
          And why not let the world enjoy
          A new kind of drama in which
          I play the love struck gallant

	You the servant footloose and free.
ALONSO:	Leave my house!
MOSCATEL:	What, right now
	Without a chance to find myself
	A new master?
ALONSO:	That's right:
	Pack your bags and go!

Enter DON JUAN.

JUAN:	What's this?
MOSCATEL:	This is me getting kicked out!
	This is my master thanking me
	For all my years of loyal service.
JUAN:	Why so harsh with Moscatel?
ALONSO:	Because the dishonest rascal,
	Has committed the worst betrayal
	The human heart can conceive:
	The most wicked act of treachery
	The human mind can imagine.
JUAN:	What's he done?
ALONSO:	He's fallen in love:
	So, I've every right to sack him
	And slander his reputation.
	For in this world there is no act
	More wicked, cunning, treacherous,
	Low and base than falling in love.
JUAN:	I think you should wish him well:
	It's said, to experience love
	Is the goal of human existence
	And why shouldn't a servant love
	I confess myself a sinner?
	There was once a master who owned
	Two, dishevelled, slapdash servants….
	And everyday he'd yell at them:
	'Layabouts, go and fall in love!'
	Because he believed that when they did
	They would come to their senses

8

     Smarten up and get some work done.
     For what feeling, or what passion,
     But love, can make a man, gracious
     Brave, generous and wise?

ALONSO: Nonsense!
     You paint a pretty picture of the
     Miracles of love, but you lie:
     For there is nothing more certain to
     Make a man miser, coward, madman
     And wretch.

JUAN: How's that?

ALONSO: I'll make my case,
     You make yours and we can judge
     Whose argument is the sounder:
     A man in love wants nothing more
     Than to give everything he owns
     To the woman he adores, and:
     In the single-minded pursuit
     Of his own selfish desire he
     Neglects his friends and his servants;
     Then he becomes miserable
     As he knows there is no virtue
     In selfishness, and that it takes
     A very special kind of miser
     To spend all his time and money
     Satisfying only his own desires.
     It's wrong to claim that love makes
     A man brave, for what man is not
     Afraid as he risks his honour
     Secretly entering the house
     Of his love? How many stout hearts
     Have melted at the prospect of
     Losing the woman of their dreams?
     How many humiliations
     Have been endured by poor fellows
     Trying to capture a new love,
     Or hold on to one that has died?

And men are driven to distraction
By the giving or withholding
Of favours, for even the most
Fashion conscious fellow keen
To make a good impression will
When he feels spurned or jealous
Take to his bed in despair and
Give up all effort to maintain
Appearances, thinking only of
Cultivating his broken heart.
So, the uncertainties of love
Make a man, a coward, a miser,
A madman and a sloven; and
Whether I'm right or wrong in this
I'll not employ a lovesick servant
Who wastes his time serving his sweet-heart
When he should be serving me.

JUAN: Don Alonso, I shan't refute
Your sophistry, for in doing so
I'd insult my own suffering
Which is a result of my love:
Was I to share my tale of grief
I fear I'd be defeated here
And I've no wish to be author
Of my own humiliation.
I came to seek your advice but
As my troubles are born of love
I will remain silent, for a man
Who'd punish a servant so harshly
For being in love is unlikely
To listen to a friend whose grief
Springs from the very same cause.

ALONSO: On the contrary, I will listen
With a most sympathetic ear,
For it is not at all the same thing
For you, Don Juan, to be in love
As this rascal of a servant,

You're noble, chivalrous and rich
Being in love is your prerogative.
What business do the poor have
Singing the noble songs of love?
Who could not be amused or amazed
At the romantic ambitions of a pauper
Who sets forth to woo his lady
Without a clean shirt on his back?
Be certain Don Juan, whatever
My attitude to love, rich or poor,
True or false, you are my friend
And as such, I'm at your service.
You, wait outside.

JUAN: Please, let him stay.
I want Moscatel to hear my tale
I come for his service your advice.

ALONSO: So, speak.

JUAN: Then listen closely,
You know already, Don Alonso,
How as a willing prisoner,
I carry the yoke of love
And draw the chariot of Venus.
So easy was her victory
I am not sure which came first
Her desire to conquer me
Or my wish to be defeated
Both seemed to happen in an instant.
You also know that the reason
For my abject surrender
Is the sovereign beauty of
That most sovereign of subjects
Dona Leonor, Enriquez
Daughter of Don Pedro Enriquez
A dear friend of my late father.
This vision of pure loveliness
This divine miracle of beauty
Is the dream to which I aspire

Is the glory I long to achieve.
Although, alas, I cannot say
I am lucky enough to deserve
Her favours, to say that would be
An impudent discourtesy
Though it's true I do receive them
I cannot say I merit them
To enjoy them is one thing
To deserve them quite another:
I live an impossible bliss
Which is no tribute to my worth
But a sign of my blessed fortune.
In this sweet state, I visit her
Borne on the wings of desire
Protected by night, applauded
By silence and befriended by
Shadows to whom I owe more
Than the sun or the light of day:
I live in the knowledge I
Endure a kind of living death
Til I can openly declare my love
And beg her father for her hand:
He, I have no doubt would
Happily marry her to me
As it would be impossible
To find a couple so in love
Who are also so suitable
In terms of both estate and birth.
The reason I haven't requested
Her hand and married her and here
We meet the hole in my happiness
The obstacle to my fulfilment
The slight pain in my pleasure,
Leonor, has an elder sister
And as a father can't marry
A second daughter before he's
Disposed of the first, I haven't

Yet approached him: were I
To ask for the hand of his daughter,
I cannot specify which one,
Custom would bind him to offer
His eldest daughter, Beatriz:
Should I reject her and ask him
Instead for Leonor then my
Interest would be known and
His suspicions now sleeping
Would be aroused and I would
Surrender the easy access
To her house which I now enjoy:
If that has not already been lost
As a result of the tragic events
That took place last night and for which
I have come to seek your help.
My friend, please, listen closely.
Beatriz is the oddest creature
Ever seen in the city of Madrid
Though beautiful and intelligent
Her looks and brains are ruined
By the strangeness of her manner.
She is so vain that she will not
Look a man in the face for fear
That the slightest glimpse of her
Might cause him to drop down dead.
She is so in love with her own
Genius that to nurture it she
Studies Latin and writes verse.
Her sense of dress is unique
She tries all fashions and discards none.
Her hair is styled at least three times
A day, but the results are
Never quite to her satisfaction.
And though these affectations are
Ridiculous they're not the worst
That title must be reserved for her

Peculiar manner of speech:
Long-winded, academic, perverse
And littered with such obscurity
She's impossible to understand
Without commentary and footnotes.
The flattery and applause she
Receives from a select group
Of admirers, have made her
So proud and haughty that she
Has rejected the god of love
And declared herself a rebel
To her empire: her pretensions
And her irritating manner
Make her so entirely unpleasant
It is hard to imagine two people
So different as these two sisters
Who are forever at war
Upon the battleground
Of their drawing room: recently,
Either from envy or mistrust
Beatriz has employed a new tactic,
She accompanies Leonor
From room to room studying
Her every action and clinging
To her so closely that she seems
The shadow to her sister's light!
Last night I went to see Leonor
Stealthily and in disguise I stood
Beneath her window I gave the sign
Leonor opened the casement
I drew close but scarcely had I
Begun to express the thoughts
Prepared but not quite memorised
My heart could no longer contain,
When Beatriz appeared behind her
Clamouring for Leonor to
Leave the window, uttering

Numerous indecipherable threats
Which seemed to me to suggest
That she intended to tell her
Father of our secret meeting.
I don't know if she recognised me
So I am anxious: afraid to know
And afraid not to know the upshot
Of this incident. I dare not
Visit the house in case our secret
Has been revealed, but it's hard
To stay away because if Beatriz
Has revealed the facts of last night
Leonor's life will be in danger.
And as it is dangerous to visit
And dangerous to stay away
I've devised another solution:
I will send this letter in secret,
It is written in another hand
And I'd like Moscatel, using
All his ingenuity and wit
To carry this letter to Ines,
Who is Leonor's chamber maid:
As he's not a member of my staff,
There's nothing for him to fear.
Don Alonso, I'd like to ask you
To give him leave to fulfil this task
And I'd like you to wait with me
In the street outside her house
For should I discover Leonor
To be in danger I will snatch her
From the house and the world be damned.
I seek your assistance in this
For though I know that you take
Delight in frivolous pleasure
I also know you to be a steadfast swordsman:
So, not as a friend do I ask you
Nor as a lover do I implore you

	But as a nobleman I beg you
	To help a man who throws himself
	In all humility at your feet.
ALONSO:	Moscatel, you will carry this letter
	To the house of Don Pedro Enriquez
	Employing whatever method
	The cunning of your wit suggests;
	And place it in the hand of the maid
	To whom Don Juan recently referred.
JUAN:	My friend, you help me so quickly.
ALONSO:	My friend, if a thing must be done
	Is it not best it be done quickly?
	Take the letter and come with us.
MOSCATEL:	*(Aside.)* This feels like a dangerous job:
	But as it's Ines I'm to find,
	Who is the mistress of my heart
	Love, inspire me, give me courage!
ALONSO:	Don Juan, lead us to her street.
JUAN:	*(Aside.)* Don Alonso is a loyal friend!
ALONSO:	*(Aside.)* These affairs are so tedious!
	'Did they hear me? Did they see me?'
	I will never court a woman
	Where any kind of risk is involved:
	I knock loudly on the front door
	And in an equally loud voice
	I make my intentions quite clear.
	Whether I'm brave or timid depends
	On one thing and one thing alone.
	Is the woman, or is she not, rich!

Exit DON ALONSO, DON JUAN and MOSCATEL.

SCENE TWO

A street outside Don Pedro's house. Enter DON JUAN, DON ALONSO, MOSCATEL.

JUAN:	This is the street! Can I suggest

> We take cover in this doorway
> So we might avoid being seen.

Enter DON LUIS and DON DIEGO.

ALONSO: Good thinking! But who are these men
           Who gaze so intently towards
           The house of Dona Leonor?

JUAN: That is Don Luis Osorio:
           Whom I have seen in this street
           Too often of late, his presence
           Has become something of a problem.

ALONSO: Why don't we go over there and
           Give him something of a problem?

JUAN: Enough! This is not the moment.
           Please, let them pass and say nothing.

ALONSO: I'm silent: do you imagine
           This puppet to be your rival?

Exit DON LUIS and DON DIEGO, tipping their hats as they exit.

JUAN: Moscatel, conceal the letter
           And carry it to Ines.

MOSCATEL: I'm frightened!

JUAN: There's no reason to be afraid,
           We will remain within earshot.
           Go inside now. Go quickly! Go.

Exit MOSCATEL, DON JUAN and DON ALONSO. Enter DON DIEGO and DON LUIS.

LUIS: Here is the bountiful sphere
           Here a remnant of heaven
           Realm of the beautiful goddess
           Home of the most perfect planet
           Ever witnessed by the sun as he
           Begins his daily journey borne
           On a tidal wave of golden fire
           To die once more, consumed
           On a bonfire of flaming ice;
           Though her beauty be ineffable

17

It is not her greatest blessing:
Had she been born ugly none would
Register such a blot beside
The blistering radiance of her mind.

DIEGO: I see, and do you approach this
Young lady with a view to marriage?

LUIS: I pay court to her and woo her
In the name of love and profit.
My family are doing the deal
With her family as we speak.

DIEGO: Are you making the right choice?

LUIS: I have found her to be a woman
Of great virtue: wealthy, noble
Beautiful and intelligent.

DIEGO: Is her intelligence too great?
I wouldn't want a wife who knew
A lot more than I did, in fact:
I'd like her to know a lot less.

LUIS: How could knowledge ever be
A hindrance?

DIEGO: When it's inappropriate!
A girl needs to know how to darn
How to spin, how to sew a patch:
She has no need to study books
Or compose exotic verse.

LUIS: She shouldn't be criticised for
Engaging in such activities,
But praised for discovering
Noble outlets, wherein she may
Express the brilliance of her wit.

DIEGO: Let me remind you these are not
The only ways she employs her wit.
I refer to the utter contempt
With which she greets your attentions.

LUIS: It's her contempt that I adore:
Shall we walk back along the street?

	I'd rather not bump into those
	Two men again they trouble me.
DIEGO:	Let's go.
LUIS:	Farewell, sweet province

Of the indifference I worship,
Soon I'll return to your threshold
For a lover who is banished
From the street of his beloved is
A creature out of his element:
Fish without water, bird without air
Beast without earth, flame without fire,
Leaf without branch, voice without breath
Body without soul, soul without heaven.

Exit DON DIEGO and DON LUIS.

SCENE THREE

The House of DON PEDRO. Enter LEONOR and INES.

LEONOR:	Has my sister finished dressing?
INES:	She's still not happy with her hair.
	I thought to myself, as she sat
	There vainly begging her mirror
	For compliments and advice,
	She might keep this going until
	I'm dead and rotting in my grave,
	So, I gave up and came in here.
LEONOR:	That mirror is a useless friend.
INES:	A useless friend, how come?
LEONOR:	When someone begs help from
	A person in a moment of need
	And that person can't come up
	With anything of much use, then
	That person is a useless friend:
	Well, my sister begs her mirror
	For help a thousand times a day
	And as it's failed so far to speak

A single word to cheer her up,
Her mirror is a useless friend.

INES: I've got it?

LEONOR: Got what?

INES: Why those two can't communicate
Your sister talks, muddy obscurity
While her mirror talks, crystal clear
That's why they never get on.

LEONOR: Oh, how lucky are they who have
So little to worry about.
My dearest Ines, I'm frightened
This infuriating prig
Is going to speak to father
This morning and tell him what she
Overheard me saying on the
Balcony last night.

INES: Let's see
The master left the house first thing
Wanting to avoid the usual rows,
So she can't have told him yet,
I'm sure we can concoct a plan
To snuff out your sister's malice.

LEONOR: I have been trying to concoct
A plan, but so far I haven't
Come up with anything useful.
It's so difficult as she saw me
On the balcony talking with
Don Juan.

INES: When a thing has been seen
It must be denied with gusto,
With real confidence and style
But when a thing hasn't seen
You just deny it with a shrug.

LEONOR: The only plan I've come up with,
My dear Ines, I can hardly speak,
Is to throw myself on her mercy

	Tell her all my hopes and dreams and
	Hope a secret shared will bind us
	Tightly behind an iron door.
INES:	A boy caught kissing his sweetheart
	By a priest used that manoeuvre,
	The priest was not a discrete man
	So the lad, sure his secret was
	About to be shared with the world
	Made an honest man of a thief,
	He went to the church and told him
	The whole story in confession
	Then the priest couldn't say a word.
LEONOR:	That's exactly my plan.
INES:	Yes, but
	A priest is bound by solemn vows.
	Is a priestess? I don't think so.
LEONOR:	That was my only solution:
	Ines, what will I do?

Enter BEATRIZ, looking at herself in a mirror.

BEATRIZ:	Excuse me!
	Is there no minion to hand?
INES:	What is your command?
BEATRIZ:	Abstract
	This bewitching crystal glass
	From my encumbered dexter
	And realise my chiroteques.
INES:	And what are chiroteques?
BEATRIZ:	Gloves!
	Shall I be required to employ
	None but the most vulgar nouns?
INES:	Thanks, next time I won't have to ask.
	Here. Gloves.

BEATRIZ:	*(Aside.)* I wage a constant war
	Against the forces of ignorance.
	Ines!
INES:	Madam?
BEATRIZ:	Retrieve,
	From my library a volume of Ovid
	Not, the *Metamorphoses*, no, no
	Nor, the *Ars Amandi*, neither
	But, the *Remedia Amoris*,
	For that is where I'll begin my
	Serious investigation.
INES:	How am I meant to fetch a book,
	If that is what you're asking for
	When I can't even read the words
	Which are written on a playbill?
BEATRIZ:	Oh, poor benighted creature
	Proud, pitiful, illiterate:
	Does daily intercourse with me
	Bring no improvement to your mind?
LEONOR:	*(Aside.)* It's time for me to play my part.
	Dear sister…
BEATRIZ:	Who summons me thus?
LEONOR:	She who in all humility
	Prostrates herself…
BEATRIZ:	Desist!
	Desire not such propinquity!
	Your proximity would sully
	The purity of my chaste bosom
	Profane the altar of my honour
	So meticulously preserved:
	She who entrusts her person to
	The shadowy chaos of night
	Shunning the honest light of day
	Pursuing nocturnal pleasure
	Shall never look upon me nor
	Expect me to lend willing ear

	To her words for she is surely
	A viper in human form whose
	Very breath would poison virtue.
LEONOR:	Wise and beautiful, Beatriz...
BEATRIZ:	I can no longer acknowledge
	You, libidinous sister!
LEONOR:	Sister!
	What is libidinous?
BEATRIZ:	She who,
	By the pale light of a street lamp,
	Tremulous viceroy of the sun,
	Dares to open casement window
	And with voice low and yet lip full
	Casts naked words beneath the moon
	Striking dumb the innocent dawn:
	But I will mitigate the shame
	With which you besmirch our house
	Making the paternal bosom privy
	To the sacrilegious nature of your faith:
	Last night I saw a devotee…
LEONOR:	Did you recognise him?
BEATRIZ:	Never!
	Impossible, have I not sworn to
	Avoid all members of that gender.
LEONOR:	I would like to tell you his name
	And with what honest intention
	He comes to speak...
BEATRIZ:	What insolence!
	I'll not permit such violation.
LEONOR:	Permitted or not you'll hear me!
	You will not ruin my good name
	With your sick fantasies which
	See shame and disgrace where there
	Is nothing but love and honour!
BEATRIZ:	Honour!
LEONOR:	Sister, listen!

BEATRIZ:	Your words,
	Will gain no access to my ear.
LEONOR:	With or without permission
	You will hear what I have to say.
BEATRIZ:	Should I be forced to listen to
	Your clandestine words I'd be
	Complicit in your conspiracy
	A sin, which I'll never commit.
LEONOR:	Listen!
BEATRIZ:	An asp, I am an asp!
	With no ear for conspiracy.
	I will not hear! I will not hear!

Exit BEATRIZ.

LEONOR:	Sister! Listen! Hear me! Who's that?
INES:	Someone come to see the master.
LEONOR:	You'd better find out what he wants.
	And though it will test my patience
	I must pursue this wilful creature.

Exit LEONOR. Enter MOSCATEL.

MOSCATEL:	*(Aside.)* Love! I'm here on your behalf.
	I'm still waiting on that courage.
INES:	Oh, god almighty, Moscatel!
	I can't believe you've got the cheek
	To show your face in this house!
MOSCATEL:	Perhaps all this hostility
	Is a little bit premature:
	You don't even know why I'm here!
INES:	You're in my house, it's a problem!
MOSCATEL:	Kind of, yes and no.
INES:	Yes and no!
MOSCATEL:	No, as you don't know why I'm here!
	Yes, as it's making you angry!
	No, as I'm going to tell you soon!
	Yes, as I'll string it out a bit!
	My dear Ines, I could have come:

24

Dragged by your divine beauty
Driven by my deep longing, or
Distracted at the thought of yours:
But I've actually come here to
Deliver a note from Don Juan,
Who has given into my care
His precious thoughts for Leonor:
He entrusted me with the job
As I'm not a member of his staff
So I can't be traced back to him
And because he knows I also
Suffer the sweet pain of love and
Would therefore make a much better
Go-between than some poor fool
Unacquainted with love's torment.

INES: Tell him, you gave me the letter
Tell him, I'll give it to Leonor,
And go, as quickly as you can
Because knowing my rotten luck
Beatriz will...

MOSCATEL: I'm out of here!
Much as I love to be near you
I will accept your curt dismissal
Deprive myself of your cruelty
In the desperate hope that my
Utter obedience might earn me
A little credit in your favour.

INES: I'd really appreciate the chance
To prove to you that I am not
As uncaring as I might appear
But just you being in this room
Is making me so nervous that
All explanations will have to
Wait for a more... Oh, my God!
My master's coming up the stairs:
There's no way he's going to see me
In this room talking to you!

25

Exit INES. Enter DON PEDRO.

MOSCATEL:	Hold on, hear me, listen up, wait!
PEDRO:	Whom do you wish to hear and wait?
	Who should hold on and listen up?
MOSCATEL:	Those to whom I might be speaking.
	Those who might be speaking for me.
PEDRO:	What are you doing here?
MOSCATEL:	*(Aside.)* Take a wild guess,
	What do you think I'm doing here?
PEDRO:	Why don't you answer?
MOSCATEL:	*(Aloud.)* I've got
	Absolutely no idea what to say!
PEDRO:	What do you want?
MOSCATEL:	*(Aside.)* What a mess!
	(Aloud.) I'm looking for my murderer.
PEDRO:	Why?
MOSCATEL:	Because not once in my life
	Have I found a single thing
	I was looking for!
PEDRO:	Who are you?
MOSCATEL:	*(Aloud.)* A servant, a humble servant.
	The enemy one can't live without.
PEDRO:	Who do you serve?
MOSCATEL:	I don't serve, sir.
	Although, I am a servant, sir.
PEDRO:	How's that?
MOSCATEL:	Because, in our house,
	I do all the mastering, whilst
	My master, sir, he serves me, sir!
PEDRO:	How dare you speak to me like this?
	I'm losing all patience with you!
MOSCATEL:	*(Aside.)* This is going really badly.
	I am about to get a kicking
	While my master's hanging about
	In a doorway doing nothing.

PEDRO: Tell me who you are, who you were
Speaking to as I came in here
And why you've entered my house;
Answer these questions directly
Or I'll draw my sword and kill you!

MOSCATEL: As you've already signed my death
Warrant and ordered my summary
Execution, I don't suppose
There's any hope of an appeal?

DON PEDRO draws his sword.

                  I'm Moscatel and my master
                  Is Don Alonso de Luna.

DON JUAN and DON ALONSO, climbing the stairs.

DON JUAN: *(Off.)* Don Pedro came through this door
Not long after Moscatel,
We must find out what's going on.

ALONSO: *(Off.)* I will do whatever's required.
Should I guard this door!

DON PEDRO: Proceed!

Enter DON JUAN.

DON JUAN: Don Pedro sir, what's going on?

MOSCATEL: *(Aside.)* At last!

DON PEDRO: *(Aside.)*   It's rather important
I appear utterly relaxed.
(Aloud.) I found this stranger in my house.
Though what he wants is far from clear.

DON JUAN draws his sword on MOSCATEL.

DON JUAN: He will confess, or he will die
On my sword!

MOSCATEL: *(Aside.)*   Thank you!

DON JUAN: *(Aside.)*   Moscatel!
Invent something, sort this out.

MOSCATEL: *(Aside.)* I'm so pleased you came to help!
(Aloud.) I came here, looking for a man,

I called, when no one answered
I climbed the stairs, step by step
Finding no one to speak to,
I entered this pleasant chamber
Where I bumped into a woman:
(Aside.) Use the truth where it's useful.
She, imagining I was a thief
Ran off, it was to her I called:
Hold on, hear me, listen up, wait!

DON JUAN: His story seems to hold water.

DON PEDRO: *(Aside.)* I am not convinced he's telling
The truth: but I should be a fool
To let Don Juan think, that I think
Something more serious is going on,
My strategy must therefore be,
To appear to believe this tale,
Then, when defences are lowered
To follow this rogue and see if
I can't put an end to my doubts!
(Aloud.) If you were searching for a man
Why were you disturbed seeing me?

MOSCATEL: Because I'm easily disturbed.

DON JUAN: Get out, and may God forgive you.

MOSCATEL: Yes, sir, may he forgive us all.

DON JUAN: *(Aside.)* Tell Don Alonso to withdraw.

Exit MOSCATEL.

DON PEDRO: Don Juan, I must leave you, farewell.

DON JUAN: Where are you going?

DON PEDRO: For a stroll!
I appear to have mislaid some
Rather important paperwork.

DON JUAN: How can I allow you to search
Without offering my support?

DON PEDRO: *(Aside.)* I must have given myself away!
He knows I'm up to something.
I'll try and throw him off the scent.

(Aloud.) Don Juan let's go together?

DON JUAN: *(Aside.)* Everything's worked out rather well.
He clearly doesn't suspect a thing.
I can leave with him without fear.

Exit DON JUAN and DON PEDRO. Enter INES.

INES: I watched that scene very closely
But I'm not sure what's going on.
He talking to himself so intensely
Yet playing it all so casually
He telling him off so sternly
But leaving with him so happy.
So many plots and counter plots
Where is this business going to end?

LEONOR: *(Off.)* Why don't you go and burn in hell!

Enter LEONOR.

INES: My lady, what on earth's happened
To put you into such a temper?

LEONOR: Beatriz! She won't listen. She's
As rude today as ever she was
Yet more selfish and arrogant
Than she has ever been before:
In short, she's going to tell father
Everything.

INES: When bad times come
They never seem to come alone,
But linked in some cruel chain, where one
Disaster lands itself in your path
Before you've got rid of the last.
When you left this room, madam,
You asked me to discover who
The strange man was that we both saw
Running up the stairs, it turns out
That man came here looking for you
With a love letter from Don Juan,
Who had sent the man here because
He didn't want to take the risk

Of sending one of his own staff:
Just as this man was handing me
The letter, it was heaven's will
That your father should walk in and
Catch the strange man in this room.
Then your Don Juan showed up and
Forced the man to come out with
The daftest excuse you ever heard,
The master tried hard to control
His feelings and be strategic,
But he couldn't quite manage it,
Then to cover up his mistake
He comes up with a daft excuse,
And rushes off into the street
In pursuit of the aforesaid man
With Don Juan fastened to his arm.

LEONOR: Disasters are like the Phoenix
If such a bird exists, the tomb
Where one vexation dies is the
Cradle in which the next is born.
Ines, give me Don Juan's letter
For I must write to him, urgently,
Telling him of the danger I'm in.

INES: Don't put it away, madam, read it.
Perhaps it contains a warning
Or something else you should know.

LEONOR: Right! Good idea. Break the seal.
Reading it can't do any harm.

INES: Your sister's here!

LEONOR: Help, heaven!

Enter BEATRIZ.

BEATRIZ: What contraband communiqué
Do you crumple and secrete?

LEONOR: Me?

BEATRIZ: You!

LEONOR: I don't understand the question.

BEATRIZ: Sister, please do not attempt
To circumvent my reasonable
Enquiry with an implausible
Excuse: I'd like to cast my eye
Upon that grubby parchment
Where with sharpened quill of goose
In ink of darkest beetle black
Drawn from well of corneous horn
Hand, has scribbled brief missive.

LEONOR: Since you're not prepared to listen
To that which I was keen to share
And would force me to reveal
That which I wish to keep concealed.
Why would I ever show you this?

BEATRIZ: Sister, as senior sibling
It's my duty to ignore your words
But pay close attention to your deeds
For the former will lie, while the latter
Speak only truth: it's appropriate
Therefore, I give no heed to that
You'd like me to hear, preferring
To reveal what you seek to conceal.

LEONOR: And if I won't give you the letter.
How will you get it?

BEATRIZ: Like this!

BEATRIZ makes a grab for the letter, they fight.

BEATRIZ: Unhand, that epistle!

INES: That's no epistle!
That's gospel!

LEONOR: Bully! Boffin! Tyrant!
You may bite and scratch me, but
I'll die before I surrender this!

BEATRIZ: Release the letter!

Enter DON PEDRO; the sisters tear the letter in half.

PEDRO: What letter?

	Why do you fight so viciously?
INES:	*(Aside.)* Why does the master always show up
	At exactly the wrong moment!
PEDRO:	You will, release this portion.
	Whilst you, release the other.
LEONOR:	*(Aside.)* Love, fill me brim full of cunning.
BEATRIZ:	The poor fragment you liberate
	From my gentle hand will reveal:
	Fatal stains upon your honour.
LEONOR:	Sir, I know nothing of the letter
	You hold in your hands, but as
	Beatriz seems so sure of its contents
	One can only assume it belongs
	To her, indeed, when I first entered
	This room she was…
BEATRIZ:	I?
LEONOR:	You!
PEDRO:	Silence!
LEONOR:	Reading the letter and having
	Become aware of what she
	Was up, to I threw myself
	Upon her in an attempt to
	Liberate the letter, she resisted,
	With some violence. My actions
	Though presumptuous, were born
	Of a genuine concern for
	The honour of our noble house:
	I must confess, I know the man
	Who writes to Beatriz, also
	Visits her on her balcony
	At night, which is why I felt
	Justified, though her junior in
	Bending the laws of decorum
	If only on this occasion.
INES:	*(Aside.)* Leonor, will always win hands down
	When they compete on equal terms.

PEDRO: Beatriz! What's this?

BEATRIZ: I'm shocked,
            By my sister's accusations
            I am bereft of words, I am
            A statue of fire and snow.
            Every crime she ascribes to me is hers
            To the word, to the letter.

LEONOR: Ines was in the room let her
            Tell us exactly what happened.

BEATRIZ: Yes, Ines was in the room
            Let her tell us, what happened.

INES: Yes, I was in this room when
            Whatever happened, happened.

PEDRO: *(Aside.)* I stand between two armies
            Each of whom is armed against me,
            Each of whom is capable of
            Destroying my reputation:
            To know which daughter is guilty
            Will bring scant relief, for
            In the bloody battle of honour
            I shall be so besieged by pain
            So harried by necessity
            So surrounded by misfortune
            That to know the face of my
            Nemesis, will not, oh heaven
            Help me to avoid my death!
            (Aloud.) Beatriz, you may leave the room
            Leonor, you may depart as well.

BEATRIZ: Sir, please allow me…

PEDRO: No more words!

LEONOR: *(Aside.)* I hope love didn't make Don Juan
            Write anything in the letter
            Which might contradict my story.

BEATRIZ: You mendacious sibling, you are
            Responsible, for everything!

Exit LEONOR and BEATRIZ.

PEDRO:	Ines. Come.
INES:	*(Aside.)* Now, it's my turn.
PEDRO:	Stay.
INES:	*(Aside.)* Who knows what I'm going to say.
PEDRO:	You were the sole witness, tell me:
	Which one was reading the letter?
INES:	*(Aside.)* I don't make the rules and I don't
	Break them: I just try to survive.
PEDRO:	Why don't you speak? Why so afraid?
INES:	*(Aside.)* In my job description it says:
	A maid should support the liar.
	(Aloud.) Sir, I arrived in this chamber
	Shortly before you and could not
	Determine by word or gesture
	To which of your daughters
	The letter belonged: I swear this
	To be true on the sacred oath
	All servants swear when they begin
	Their lives of dedicated service.
PEDRO:	*(Aside.)* It seems I am to be denied
	Even the meagre balm that
	Knowing might have brought.
	Ines. Leave.
INES:	*(Aside.)* Well played, Ines, well played.

Exit INES.

PEDRO:	The letter will reveal what she
	And they would like to keep hidden.
	I must now cleave two fragments
	Of a viper, a deadly snake
	Whose venom is contained in both.

DON PEDRO reconnects the two halves of the letter and reads.

            'Beautiful beloved, it's hard
            For me to quantify or express
            The feelings that have engulfed me
            Since your sister overheard us

Last night. Let me know the moment
She tells your father, so I might
Carry you to a place of safety'.
These words could apply to either
So, my misery is increased,
For if I knew which was loose
At least I'd know which was honest,
But that must not be, for heaven
Has ordained I must believe
Neither and yet suspect them both.
I met a man who was disturbed,
Oh God, to see me in this room
Don Juan arrived I let the man go
I follow him, I lose track of him,
I come home and am confronted
By an intrigue I can't resolve!
All these matters demand calm
And careful consideration.
I have learnt that the stranger serves
(Unless his fear made him a liar)
One, Don Alonso de Luna,
My goal must be to know him better
To shadow his every action!
Until I've proof of my disgrace
And have conceived my revenge,
Patience, heaven, give me patience.

ACT TWO

SCENE ONE

A street in Madrid. Enter DON JUAN, DON ALONSO and MOSCATEL.

ALONSO: We were lucky to escape!

MOSCATEL: I was lucky to escape!
In fact, I was unlucky
To be in there in the first place:
I was staring death in the face!

DON JUAN: Moscatel, you were fortunate,
That I seized the initiative
And followed Don Pedro upstairs.

MOSCATEL: Don Juan you were fortunate!
If you'd arrived any later
I'd have confessed the whole story!

ALONSO: Would you, indeed?

MOSCATEL: Indeed, I would!
And as fast as my mouth could spit
Out the words.

ALONSO: You see, Don Juan
Love has made another coward!

DON JUAN: Has love made us cowards?

MOSCATEL: And worse!
Because the life a lover risks,
Is not his own to play with
But is pledged in the service
Of his beloved, it is therefore
A very fraudulent business
For him to mortgage that life
To settle another man's debt.

ALONSO: For Don Juan's sake I've put up
Your ridiculous nonsense,
Listened to your dreary tales of

Pleasure and pain, but now,
As there seems to be if not a truce
At least a lull in hostilities,
It's time for you to tell us something
More entertaining, having heard
The romantic drivel, it's time
We derived a little pleasure
From this tryst, so, you will tell us
The name of your secret sweetheart
And how far have you got with her.

MOSCATEL: I might tell you how far I've got
But I'll never tell you her name.

ALONSO: What makes you so distrustful?

MOSCATEL: You!

DON JUAN: But you trust me?

MOSCATEL: I trust no one!

ALONSO: How far have you got with her?

MOSCATEL: I've cause to hope that one day soon
The destiny of our pure love
Will reach an honest fulfilment.

ALONSO: You know sometimes, I could slap
Your ugly face, Don Juan, tell me
How much longer must I listen
To the ramblings of this blockhead!
The destiny of their pure love?
The mop girl and the errand boy!

Enter INES, covered in a shawl, with a letter.

INES: Don Juan! Sir!

DON JUAN: Who's that?

INES: It's me, sir!

INES lifts her shawl, revealing her face.

DON JUAN: Welcome, Ines!

INES: I've been running
Up and down the streets of Madrid
Looking for you.

37

DON JUAN:	What's happened?
MOSCATEL:	*(Aside.)* My darling Ines! God in heaven I'm begging, don't let my master Catch the smallest glimpse of her.
INES:	I came to give you this letter. Goodbye.
JUAN:	Stop, Ines. Wait. I will read it now.

As DON JUAN reads, MOSCATEL places himself between DON ALONSO and INES.

ALONSO:	Before heaven A very attractive young lady!
MOSCATEL:	*(Aside.)* He's seen her! Oh, my honour Isn't worth a rotten penny now.
ALONSO:	Moscatel! Come here!
MOSCATEL:	Yes, master.
ALONSO:	If this beauty were your sweetheart I might forgive your falling in love. If such a crime could be forgiven.
MOSCATEL:	*(Aside.)* Jealousy, let's take this slowly. Don't knock me out with the first punch. *(Aloud.)* You really think she's good looking?
ALONSO:	I think she's very attractive. For a mop girl.
MOSCATEL:	I disagree! I think she's ugly, plain ugly. If you saw my girl you wouldn't Give this one a second glance. She might give you something that one.
ALONSO:	Moscatel, you're lying to me!
DON JUAN:	I read it.
ALONSO:	What does it say?
DON JUAN:	A thousand worries and complaints. But I'm under no suspicion And may visit her at leisure

Due to some ruse she's invented
Of which she says very little.
I will go now and seek you out
When I've done: Ines, let's go.

Exit DON JUAN and INES.

ALONSO: Moscatel!
             Don't let her get away, stop her!

MOSCATEL: *(Aside.)* Jealousy! I give up!

ALONSO: Sweetheart!

INES: What do you want?

ALONSO: I'd love to see
             Your pretty face.

MOSCATEL: *(Aside.)*   Heaven, help me!

INES: My face deserves close scrutiny,
             But sadly sir, I am in a rush.

ALONSO: I'll only steal a tiny glance.

MOSCATEL: *(Aside.)* He'll steal her maidenhead as fast.

Enter DON LUIS and DON DIEGO.

DIEGO: Isn't that her maid, over there.

LUIS: *(Aside.)* We saw her leave Don Pedro's house
             And followed closely so I might
             Pass her a note for Beatriz.

INES: *(Aside.)* Moscatel is making signs at me.
             But I've no idea what they mean.

DIEGO: She is in deep conversation
             With Don Alonso de Luna.

DON LUIS: Which confirms all my suspicions:
             Her maid comes out in search of him,
             He is constantly in her street
             Beneath her window with his friend,
             Her maid hangs back to engage him
             In private conversation after
             His friend's most hasty departure.
             Everything points in one direction.

DON DIEGO: Which is?

DON LUIS: A secret love affair.

DIEGO: What will you do?

LUIS: I shall withdraw.
I've no desire to be seen here:
My advances have been spurned
I have been granted no favours
And to draw a sword in the name
Of a woman who has shown me
Nothing but scorn strikes me as a
Very foolish kind of valour.

DIEGO: I agree with your reasoning
But perhaps the base jealousy
Which is laying siege to your brain,
Is misleading you in this instance.

LUIS: Diego, jealousy is never base.

DEIGO: Many people would disagree!

LUIS: Is there a more noble attribute
Than speaking the truth? There is not!
Jealousy is god's greatest gift
For the jealous man never lies!

Exit DON DIEGO and DON LUIS.

INES: Yes, right. I have to go. Goodbye.

ALONSO: I shan't let you walk home alone.
Let my man escort you.

INES: Why not!
Let your servant take me home.

MOSCATEL: *(Aside.)* What's this I hear? What's this I see?

ALONSO: Moscatel!

MOSCATEL: Master!

ALONSO: Over here!
Ines has given her permission
For you to escort her on my behalf
Back to her house, so take her arm:
On the way you will let her know
That should she pay me a visit

She'd not leave without a present.

MOSCATEL: And you'd like me to tell her that?

ALONSO: I would, you see, it's important
That while I'm helping Don Juan
Through his romantic tribulations
I generate my own projects
To keep myself happy and amused.

MOSCATEL: I'll tell her, so.

ALONSO: I'll be waiting
In this tavern for her reply.

Exit DON ALONSO.

MOSCATEL: *(Aside.)* Oh, honour! What a way to lose you!

INES: So, Moscatel, let's go! Come on.
What's wrong?

MOSCATEL: Nothing, Ines. Let's go.

INES and MOSCATEL exit the stage and re-enter.

INES: You can't lift your eyes from the ground?
Is taking me home such a bore?
What's up?

MOSCATEL: My, beautiful, Ines.
Oh, sweet enchantress of my soul.
What terrible pain you cause me.

INES: What's the matter?

MOSCATEL: Love is the matter.
My honour is the matter!
I am both a lover and servant
And today I must make a choice:
To stop serving? To stop loving?

INES: I don't understand what you're saying.

MOSCATEL: Then, let me explain. My master,
Don Alonso, has seen you, Ines,
Though I wish it had pleased heaven
To strike him blind before he had,
He saw you and in seeing you
Oh, God! In the very moment his

41

Eyes embraced you, he fell in love,
Not with your infinite beauty
But with his own very finite plans
For that beauty: in short Ines
You're the next new face in town.
He asked me to escort you home
So I might, oh, my mouth's run dry
The words stick fast in my throat,
So, that I might tell you, Ines,
If you were to go to his house
He would reward you, oh the shame,
For a morning visit, breakfast
And supper if you spend the night!
I know it's a terrible disgrace
For a man: I am a volcano!
To play pimp: I am Mount Etna!
To his sweetheart, but is it not
Also a disgrace for a servant
To be disloyal to his master?
So, torn between two obligations
I will do my duty and declare:
He loves you! He desires you!
Having delivered the bitter truth
Let my jealous torment begin
In the moment your joy is born.

INES: You ill bred, uncouth, lunatic!
You will hold that wicked tongue!
What have you seen in me makes you
Think you can speak to me like that?
You can go and tell your master,
Peasant: that I am who I am,
That he can forget any plans
He might have for me; that I'll
Not be paying him any visits,
That I'm not one of those poor sluts
Who's paid breakfasts and suppers
That I'm a woman with a mind

	Of her own, I go my own way!
	You go and tell your master that!
MOSCATEL:	That's your answer!
INES:	That's my answer!
	And get yourself off home, sharpish
	I don't want anyone to see you here.
	Look, we're right outside my house.
MOSCATEL:	It's hard to go, we haven't made up.
INES:	Don't follow me. Don't speak to me.
MOSCATEL:	I hear your orders and I obey.
	But I'll leave with a heavy heart.
	'Eyes, drop tears, on sad cheeks
	It's no disgrace, for you to weep.'

Exit MOSCATEL.

INES:	Here's the house. I'd best remove
	This shawl before I go inside.
	See the real reason why we wear
	These farthingales under our skirts.
	They hide a multitude of sins.
	Now although my silly mistress
	Might have missed me she will
	Never guess I've been outside,
	As long as I can trust you lot,
	Not to tell her where I've been:
	Word of honour, you keep it shut.

SCENE TWO

The house of Don Pedro.

Enter DON JUAN and LEONOR and then INES.

LEONOR:	And that was the lie which freed us
	From a very tricky situation.
JUAN:	As it was conceived by your wit
	It is a lie which I adore.
LEONOR:	With my whole life in the balance

I came up with a story which
Has at least given us some respite.
It's no mean achievement to make
That which was crystal clear, muddy.

JUAN: Now your father suspects you both?

LEONOR: He's on a mission, following
Us both about the house, creeping
From room to room attempting to listen in
On our conversations, but as yet
He has no idea who wrote the letter
Or for whom it was meant, Ines,
Who is witness to all my crimes
Sowed seeds of doubt in his mind.

INES: I didn't say the letter belonged
To Beatriz, in case the contents
Caught me out, but I said nothing
To contradict your story.

DON JUAN: If my memory serves me right
I seem to recall the letter
Being written in such a way
The contents could apply to either,
That I didn't address it to you
And had it written in another hand?
But tell me, how is Beatriz
Coping with being a suspect?

LEONOR: She's so in love with
Her immaculate reputation
That being under suspicion
Is driving her to distraction.
She wanders the house like a ghost
Talking to herself and sobbing,
I am overjoyed to see her
Like this and would be delighted
If we could come up with a way
To make real, this phantom love
Which I invented for her and for
Which She suffers so terribly.

INES: Sir, can you suggest a method
                    Which might help us to increase
                    Her discomfort?

LEONOR: Thank you, Ines.
                    Don Juan, it would be very much
                    To our advantage in this battle
                    If we could sustain the black cloud
                    Of suspicion which hangs over
                    My dear sister and who knows
                    It might stop her bullying me
                    And silence her ridiculous tongue.

DON JUAN: I'll be your sword of vengeance!
                    I'll bring a certain friend of mine
                    To visit Beatriz who will pretend
                    To fall in love with, here she comes.
                    I will tell you more of this anon,
                    For the moment, I will say nothing.

LEONOR: Come, she shouldn't see you here
                    For though there's no suspicion
                    Attached to your name we must
                    Be very careful in all our dealings

JUAN: Leonor, the beautiful, farewell.

INES: In the name of Spain and Saint James,
                    Let's go and sort her out. Come on.

Exit INES, LEONOR and DON JUAN.

SCENE THREE

The house of Don Pedro. Enter BEATRIZ.

BEATRIZ: Like the solitary Phoenix, I come
                    With no companion but my thoughts,
                    To examine in soliloquy
                    The nature of my unhappiness
                    And the blighted horoscope
                    Under which I must drag out my days.
                    My honour, the glorious sun

Which illuminates my world,
Suffers a painful eclipse,
As an opaque planet on an
Erratic epicycle has
Placed itself between myself
And the precious light casting
My days into darkness: I refer
To the lies of Leonor…

LEONOR: Did you summon me?

BEATRIZ: You would be wrong to think
That though in solitude I spoke
Your name, this act represents
Any desire on my behalf
To call you to my presence.
If naming were summoning
I might banish my torments by
Merely naming their opposite.

LEONOR: Why in solitude do you speak
My name with such contempt?

BEATRIZ: Why need you ask the question?
But let your own mendacity
Be it's punishment dear sister:
Was it not you, in the name of love
To whom the letter was sent?

LEONOR: Yes.

BEATRIZ: And was it not you who mislead
Our progenitor with the
Falsehood that the lineated paper
Was intended for me?

LEONOR: Yes.

BEATRIZ: And was it not you who made
This falsehood so convincing
That truth herself was confounded
And purity defiled?

LEONOR: Yes, Beatriz.

BEATRIZ: Then how can you be surprised

	When I lament your fraudulence?
LEONOR:	See what your spite has achieved!
	Would I have invented the lie
	If you had helped keep my secret?
	Of course not, but when war broke out
	I had no choice but to defend
	My own position: in front of you
	I'll not deny I told a lie
	But I'll never confess as much
	In front of another person.
	I love, I adore, I die of love…
	(Aside.) God in heaven, it's my father.

LEONOR sees DON PEDRO, he withdraws behind a curtain.

DON PEDRO:	*(Aside.)* 'I die of love' I heard her say!
LEONOR:	*(Aside.)* With a slight change of inflection
	I can soon correct my mistake,
	'I die of love?' You say to me!
	'I, love?'
DON PEDRO:	*(Aside.)* What's this I'm seeing?
LEONOR:	'I adore'.
DON PEDRO:	What's this I'm hearing?
LEONOR:	'I die of love': in heaven's name,
	That such words should be spoken
	By a woman of your breeding!
	I've no choice but to tell father:
	And as you so recently swore
	You would confess your crime to me
	But never in his presence,
	I'll go and tell him this instant!
BEATRIZ:	Where are you going?
LEONOR:	Desist!
	Desire not such propinquity.
BEATRIZ:	It's hard to comprehend your thoughts
	You oscillate so violently.
LEONOR:	Such proximity would sully
	The purity of my chaste bosom.

BEATRIZ:	What change is this?
LEONOR:	What insolence!
	I'll not permit this violation!
PEDRO:	*(Aside.)* Leonor, is the virtuous one!
BEATRIZ:	Sister, listen!
LEONOR:	Sister, no more!
	I can no longer acknowledge
	A sister, libidinous!

Exit LEONOR.

BEATRIZ:	Whoever heard such an outburst!
	Whoever witnessed such passions!
	Such reversals! Contradictions!
PEDRO:	I did, Beatriz, oh yes, I did!
	Notice the vigilance with which
	I have shadowed you both,
	Has not been a labour in vain.
BEATRIZ:	Father, were you there all the time?
PEDRO:	Oh, yes, Beatriz, I was here.
BEATRIZ:	So, you heard Leonor's words?
PEDRO:	Oh yes, I heard Leonor's words!
BEATRIZ:	So, your mistaken sense of me
	Has been corrected?
PEDRO:	Yes it has!
	I now have solid proof your sister
	Had a perfect right chastise you!
BEATRIZ:	I can no longer be surprised!
	I was born under a cruel star.
	Oppressed by a brutal fate
PEDRO:	What brutal fate and what cold star?
BEATRIZ:	Sir, if I might...
PEDRO:	Enough! Beatriz! Enough!
	Enough of these affectations
	They are an enemy to you:
	Must I be the one to tell you
	A cunning enemy that will

Destroy your reputation!
I've learnt from recent events,
She who'll not speak as others speak
Will not behave as others behave!
I've learnt the name of the man
Who wrote you that fatal letter,
A glib and most unpleasant person.
And I've leant from Leonor's scolding
That you are in love with this rake.
Perhaps we share the blame for this
But let me assure you daughter
The remedy will be mine alone:
From today all reading ends
From today writing poetry stops
All books in Latin will be burnt:
You will make do with a simple
Book of common prayer, in Spanish
Which is all the reading matter
A respectable woman needs.
Needle work and embroidery
Will be your sole recreation,
Leave learning and study to men
And please do not look so amazed:
I will murder you if I hear you
Employ a single word or phrase
Which is not in common usage.

BEATRIZ: In obedient humility
Like the respectful sunflower.
I shall follow to the letter
All your instructions and vow
From this day never to employ,
Elevated or exotic language.
But, dear sir, I beg, grant reason
The chance to reveal to you
The many falsehoods which deceit
Has presented as evidence:
Let truth challenge the injustice

49

	With which malice is attempting
	To debilitate your benevolence!
PEDRO:	So much for your vow, Beatriz!
BEATRIZ:	In the name of consanguinity!
PEDRO:	You will drive me to distraction!

Exit DON PEDRO and BEATRIZ, separately.

SCENE FOUR

A street in Madrid. Enter DON ALONSO and MOSCATEL.

ALONSO:	The little scrubber said that?
MOSCATEL:	She said: 'Inform your master
	He'll never prevail upon me,
	I'm too moral to be his mistress
	And too low born to be his wife'.
ALONSO:	But this is the kind of reply
	Kings receive in plays from
	The Duchess of Amalfi, or
	Mantua, or Milan, it's not
	The reply that one expects from
	Her Highness the Countess of Mop.
	You know this could get interesting
	For there's nothing that excites more
	Than a mop girl playing hard to get:
	The Devil take the little minx
	She should count herself fortunate
	To be sought by a gentleman
	Who actually owns his own shirt.
MOSCATEL:	Those who wear the same linen, sir:
	Always seem to stick together.
ALONSO:	Ines, has stung me!
MOSCATEL:	Is she so sharp?
ALONSO:	And to get my revenge on her
	I mean to bed her. Go to her again.
MOSCATEL:	Me?
ALONSO:	You!

MOSCATEL: *(Aside.)* Jealousy, too soon
I bid you, farewell.

ALONSO: And tell her…

Enter DON JUAN.

JUAN: Don Alonso, thanks be to God
Today I can bring you good news,
If only to prove that love is not
Always beset by woes for today
All the trouble, the pain and grief
Have passed and the sweet the face
Of the boy love which yesterday
Was wet and covered with tears
Is today glowing with laughter.
Yesterday, I asked you to lend me
Your courage and bravery
In a serious matter of honour
Today, my fortune has improved
And I wish to avail myself of your
Courtly grace, your wit, and good taste
Then you will know in equal measure
The extremes of my joy and woe.

ALONSO: This sounds good, what happened?

JUAN: Carefully and cunningly, Leonor
Shifted the blame for all her crimes
Onto Beatriz, now Don Pedro
Can't make up his mind which daughter
Is the virtuous one and which
The malicious schemer, for that
Which seemed clear has been blurred
and it's one sister's word against
the other's, I promised to help Leonor
The wars fought between siblings
Would seem to be the most intense
And she asked me to recruit a friend
who will pretend to be in love
with Beatriz, it's important

For our campaign that she be both
Incriminated and distracted.
You are the man to be her lover
Leonor, has devised a strategy
To get you safely into the house,
So, from today, you will visit her
Worship her, bribe her chamber maid
Shadow her wherever she goes
Write her letters…

ALONSO: Stop! I will not
Talk to her, woo her, pursue her
Or even look upon her, I swear.
I, gaze up at her window
Like a lovesick clown
Whispering ardent declarations
Until a pail of cold water
Is emptied on my fond head?
I, give good money to a maid
To tell her mistress of my pain?
I, stalk a woman to find out
Where, or if, she goes to mass?
Do you think I'm the kind of man
Who writes polite love letters
Which perforce exclude all passion
And truth and are instead full of
Sweet affection and blessed bliss?
I, stand shivering all night
Beneath her window hoping
I might get a chance to hold her hand?
And listen to the old excuse
'I'm saving myself for my husband'
And yet everyday to have her
Maidenhead thrust in my face?
As God is my witness, I'll die
Before I beg, or stalk, or plead,
Gaze upon, or write love letters!
I refuse to have any dealings

With a woman unless it is clear,
That I come and go as I please
Accepting a chair on my first visit
A stool on my second and on
The third cushions, and her lap,
as the pillow for my head which
should it ever itch, she scratches.
And please, consider if you will
The prize you offer, a boffin
Blue stocking, who speaks in such
A silly and affected manner
It's impossible to comprehend her
Without recourse to a dictionary.
If there is an honest quarrel
In which I may be of service
You shall not lack my support
But before god in heaven I swear
I'd rather do battle with a
Dozen illiterate men than woo
One over-educated woman.
The women I have dealings with
Sign a contract before witnesses
Swearing they are illiterate,
Down to earth and simply spoken.

JUAN: Don Alonso it is common practice
In the court of Madrid For a
Nobleman to help a dear friend
by paying suit To his beloved's
best friend?

ALONSO: It's also common practice
For such a nobleman to lose
All he has by taking part in
Such ridiculous lotteries.

JUAN: I'm not asking you to love her
I am asking you to act the part,
You'd be merely playing a game.

ALONSO: The notion of playing a prank

On that vain and ridiculous
Madwoman is rather appealing.

MOSCATEL: *(Aside.)* How quickly he changes his mind.
All kinds of madness will be unleashed.

ALONSO: I agree: as long as it is known
To all, the whole thing is a joke:
To imagine I could woe her
In earnest, or listen, in truth
To her nonsense, would be
To imagine the impossible.

JUAN: I'm not asking you to do that.

ALONSO: From this moment I am in love.

JUAN: We must go directly to her house,
On route I tell you the details
Of the plan and let you know
How to gain access to her room
And what to say to her.

ALONSO: Let's go,
It is rather amusing to think
That my bogus wooing might
Provoke true love in Beatriz.

MOSCATEL: Well, let us hope it doesn't all
End in tears.

ALONSO: Tears? What tears, rascal!
The whole enterprise is fiction?
I am helping my friend Don Juan,
Avenging the divine Leonor,
Making a fool of Beatriz, while
Having a little fun with Ines.

Exit DON JUAN and DON PEDRO.

MOSCATEL: *(Aside.)* A little fun for him heartbreak for me.

Exit MOSCATEL.

SCENE FIVE

The house of Don Pedro. A room with a cupboard.

Enter BEATRIZ and INES.

INES: Your melancholy is great, my lady.

BEATRIZ: How could it be otherwise and more, 'tis mine?
And have I not great reason, when in consequence
Of the deceitful proclivities of Leonor
I stand calumniated before my progenitor?
How could it be imagined, I might love a man
When in this matter, I am the very definition
Of disdain! How could it be countenanced I might:
Listen to a lover's pleas, accept his letters,
Or grant him access to my private chamber
Opening a casement window at midnight
And permit him intimate contact with my dexter?
How? When even the notion of such behaviour
Dare not visit the unspotted bastion of my mind!
From hence, this sad hermitage: into which the rays
Of the sun barely penetrate, must provide
The lugubrious sphere, where: feigning life, I die:
This, the humble retreat where mocking death I live!
And the sun: at its birth, a bright narcissus of carmine
And cochineal, unto its death in the cold paroxysm
Of night, when it must greet its own reflection:
Shall never again behold my face! Unless, perchance
Some maverick atom should steal its way into
This melancholy domain in which the violation
Of my reputation requires me to take refuge.
Eyes, drop your tears, you are the compound
                              synonyms
Of my anguish and distress, provoked by the sins
Of another but blamed unjustly upon myself!
Ines, do I not lament in humble style
With a goodly composure and restraint?
Had my progenitor heard me, would he not
Praise the moderation of my language?

INES:	I'm sure he would my lady, but there are Still a few words you might like to avoid.
BEATRIZ:	Tell me, which words or phrases?
INES:	Well, I heard: Deceitful proclivities, calumniated, Unspotted bastion, lugubrious sphere, Narcissus of carmine and cochineal Cold paroxysm, compound synonyms, And a few others I can't recall just now.
BEATRIZ:	Such stultification will unhinge my wits! Are these not simple words, exchanged By every doorman in the city? So, I promise Henceforth, to clothe my cheerless thoughts In the humble clogs of common parlance, Not the elevated buskins of high tragedy.
INES:	*(Aside.)* She's doing her best.
BEATRIZ:	And should I utter Any word or phrase which might be considered Inappropriate on the lips of a lowly woman, I should like you to pluck upon the sleeve of my gown.
INES:	I accept your commission, my lady I will gladly play censor to your speech.

Enter LEONOR, DON ALONSO and MOSCATEL.

LEONOR:	*(Aside to ALONSO.)* There's Beatriz, sad and lonely Waiting for a lover to call. You may begin your performance And to ensure that you are not Interrupted I will be outside With Don Juan, we've got your back.
ALONSO:	*(Aside.)* Who'd have thought I'd be lost for words When this love is merely a charade?
INES:	Moscatel, what going on?
MOSCATEL:	The medicine is about to be administered.
INES:	I mean, why are you here?
MOSCATEL:	Why? Because

	I love you and my master's not getting near you
	Without me standing guard.
BEATRIZ:	Ines, what's this?
INES:	This, my lady, is a man
	Who has come to call upon you.
BEATRIZ:	*(Aside to INES.)* In my *cubiculo*!
	What are you doing?
INES:	*(Aside to BEATRIZ.)* Plucking your sleeve.
BEATRIZ:	*(Aside to INES.)* Stop it!
	Don't be silly, I meant of course, my room!
ALONSO:	Oh, beautiful, Beatriz.
	Waste not your words upon the air
	Don't let such sighs escape to heaven
	Rushing from the ruby prison of your lips.
	I implore you, if you can
	To rise above righteous anger
	Take pity on a lover's dreams
	Consider, cruelty may not
	Be the only legacy of beauty.
BEATRIZ:	You seem a little overfond
	Of multiple metaphor.
INES:	*(Aside to BEATRIZ.)* That's worth two plucks!
BEATRIZ:	*(Aside to INES.)* Enough!
	Rude and reckless gentleman
	You dare to violate the cloister
	Wherein the sun himself
	Who is both phoenix and pyre
	If perchance he boldly enters
	Departs meekly and if the sun
	Himself dare enter here only on
	Pretext of bringing in the dawn
	If the even atoms of that star
	Are fearful to approach me
	What insolence and audacity
	Govern your treacherous step?
	What insane passion propels

Your reckless bark so far off course
To navigate the dangerous deeps
That rational pilot never ploughed?
Headless mariner, believe this:
In the quicksand of my modesty
On the Scylla of my disdain
The Charybdis of my honour.
Your vessel will flounder and you
Yourself founder and be drowned.

INES: *(Aside.)* It's time he began to spin his lies

MOSCATEL: *(Aside.)* My master's no stranger to lying.

ALONSO: Beatriz, most learned, most wise
Beatriz, sweet enigma in whom
Such glorious eloquence might
Be considered wholly redundant for a
Deity of such surpassing beauty.
Do not be astonished that I sail,
Inspired by your divine grace
Ignoring all perils of the deep
Into these unchartered waters
For here I discover balmy waves.

INES: *(Aside.)* Moscatel, ought to pluck his sleeve!

ALONSO: For two years I have followed you
Like a sunflower, feasting on
The light of your numinous beauty
Fragrant in your blessed presence
Wilting in your cursed absence
Seeing you, my lady, is my life
And missing you that is my death.

INES: *(Aside.)* Women, watch this carefully,
Because if that was pretending
How are we to know the difference
Between a lover and a liar?

ALONSO: I believe the cause of today's
Troubles is that yesterday
Your father intercepted my man
In the act of bringing you a letter.

I am painfully aware both
Of the obligation my actions
Have placed upon me and the
Danger in which they place you.
I have taken the very first
Available opportunity
To come and offer you protection.

BEATRIZ: Sir, stop there, for it is vital
For me to ascertain precisely:
Though in doing so I risk
Breaking the laws of honour,
To which letter and to which
Servant you refer?

ALONSO: Which servant?
Why madam this servant here!
And the letter is the letter
Which though intended for you
Was wrongly opened by Leonor,
When given to her by this maid.

INES: I'm sorry. I didn't give it
She took it, without asking.

BEATRIZ: And the servant was yours?

ALONSO: Yes.

BEATRIZ: And the letter was from you?

ALONSO: Yes.

BEATRIZ: And meant for me?

ALONSO: Can you doubt me?

BEATRIZ: No, sir, I do not doubt, but know,
Feelingly, that you are the man
Who has destroyed my peace of mind
That you are the cruel tyrant
Who has tarnished the once spotless
Mirror of my sacred honour
I know, very well I should like you:
Be it in the name of mercy
Or in the name of courtesy

	To go, turn back, retrace your steps
	For should my sister find you here
	You'd bring about my death, as
	Yesterday's lies become today's truth.
INES:	*(Aside.)* See how quickly she believed him
	When I added my bit to the tale.
MOSCATEL:	*(Aside.)* Doesn't this just go to show:
	That fooling a woman is easy!
BEATRIZ:	Do you wish to inflict further
	Damage upon my vanity?
	You see, I shed tears on your account
	But know, though a man provoke tears,
	They are not a sure sign of love.
	Go.
ALONSO:	*(Aside.)* There is nothing I'd like more.
	I'm loosing my mind standing here
	With no idea what to say.
BEATRIZ:	Bring no further shame on my house
	Let it be enough, that you are
	The first man to address me in
	The dread words of concupiscence.

INES pulls at her sleeve.

	Will you stop plucking at my sleeve!
	It seems you'll not be satisfied
	Til I'm entirely mute.
ALONSO:	In faith
	And courtesy I shall withdraw,
	Allowing my planet to pursue
	Another orbit which perforce must
	Carry me away from your light
	But I can only depart when I know
	You are acquainted with my love.
BEATRIZ:	Then, sir, goodbye, I know it well.
ALONSO:	*(Aside to MOSCATEL.)* I think that started rather well.
MOSCATEL:	*(Aside to ALONSO.)* It's about to end rather badly.
	Someone's coming.

INES:	Oh, my lady,
	Don't let him go!
BEATRIZ:	Why not, Ines?
INES:	Listen, can't you hear, Leonor
	With Don Juan and your father?
MOSCATEL:	*(Aside.)* Why does that man always turn up
	At exactly the wrong moment?
BEATRIZ:	Sir, if you are discovered here
	This day will be my climacteric,
	It has pleased heaven to
	Implicate me in a number
	Of crimes of which I've never dreamed.
	My father must pass through this room
	On his way upstairs to his own, so
	You cannot go this way or that
	So, before he arrives we must
	Find you somewhere to hide, in here!
ALONSO:	It's as if we're in a comedy
	By Calderón de la Barca
	Where there's always a concealed
	Lover, or a veiled lady.
BEATRIZ:	Good sir, my honour is at stake!
ALONSO:	But do I really have to hide?
BEATRIZ:	I'd be forever in your debt.
ALONSO:	*(Aside.)* Heaven, do you think this is fair:
	To punish me with actual pain
	When the pleasure was all pretend?
BEATRIZ:	What's stopping you?
ALONSO:	What's stopping me?
	I'm waiting for you to tell me
	Where you would like me to hide.
INES:	The best place to hide is in here.
	The china cupboard.
BEATRIZ:	Good idea!
ALONSO:	The china cupboard? With the
	Cups and saucers!

BEATRIZ:	It's essential!
INES:	Squeeze in here!
ALONSO:	It's impossible!
	Unless someone has a shoehorn?
INES:	Your turn!
MOSCATEL:	Is this cupboard a two-seater,
	Like one of those mules you can hire?
INES:	Shut up and don't break the china!

The cupboard is closed, the sound of breaking china.

Enter, DON PEDRO, LEONOR and DON JUAN.

DON PEDRO: Ines, we need some light in this house.

DON JUAN: *(Aside.)* God in heaven, what will I do
If Don Pedro finds Don Alonso?
The awful truth is, I pushed him
To do this favour as a friend,
And as a friend he agreed to help.
But if we bump into him now
There is no way I can help him!

LEONOR: *(Aside.)* I wish I had never thought of
Getting back at my sister!
What began as a silly joke
Has become an awful nightmare.

PEDRO: Don Juan, just out of interest:
What time do you retire?

JUAN: Oh, early!
(Aside.) That was his rather subtle way
Of inviting me to go home,
And I of course must take the hint
If I go, I abandon my friend
But staying here is not an option:
I will go downstairs, wait outside
And monitor developments!
(Aloud.) Goodnight.

PEDRO: Goodnight, Don Juan, goodnight.
Ines, bring the light here, Don Juan is leaving.

JUAN: You don't need to escort me, sir.

PEDRO: I know exactly what must be done.

Exit DON PEDRO, DON JUAN and INES.

LEONOR: *(Aside.)* I wonder where Beatriz
                  Has hidden Don Alonso?
                  He's nowhere to be seen.

BEATRIZ: *(Aside.)* How many torments must I endure
                  For a man I don't even know?

Enter DON PEDRO with INES and the light.

PEDRO: Ines, carry the light in my room.

LEONOR: *(Aside.)* Now father will find Don Alonso
                  Who must be hiding upstairs!

PEDRO: Come with me both of you, I'd like
                  To speak to you...

China breaks in the cupboard.

PEDRO: What was that?

INES drops the candlestick.

INES: A candlestick, sir!
          I dropped it.

PEDRO: Ines, please, focus
          On the job in hand!

INES: I'm focused, sir!

Exit DON PEDRO and LEONOR.

BEATRIZ: Ines, now that my father has
                  Retired to his room, will you
                  Show our visitors to the door?
                  Leonor must not find them here!

INES: Leonor, is not the problem!
                  The master didn't go downstairs
                  With Don Juan to be a good host
                  He went downstairs to lock the door.

BEATRIZ: Well, they can't stay in the cupboard.
                  Think of something! They have to go!

Exit BEATRIZ.

INES: *(Aside.)* I know how to get rid of them.
    (Aloud.) Cupboard dwellers, time to unfold!

ALONSO: You oaf, I swear, if I had any
    Feeling in my arms, I'd kill you.

MOSCATEL: It's not my fault the china broke, it's
    In the nature of china to break!

INES: Quick, get out!

ALONSO: Ah, the angel, Ines.
    Had this drama been for your sake
    The torment would have been worthwhile.

MOSCATEL: Worthwhile? Rubbish! Worthless. Worthless!

ALONSO: Moscatel? It's time we left, but...
    Why waste a moment for romance.

DON ALONSO embraces INES, they kiss.

MOSCATEL: *(Aside.)* You must have seen the paintings of
    Saint Agnes embracing the lamb:
    Well, here's the blessed Saint Ines
    Embracing a man, while the lamb
    Stands by watching and says nothing.

INES: Time to go!

ALONSO: Show me the way!

INES: The masters locked the door downstairs.
    But there is another way out.
    Climb up here, as quickly as you can,
    Then squeeze through the window
    Drop onto the balcony and jump
    Down into the street: what's wrong?

ALONSO: First you stuff me in a cupboard
    Then hurl me off a balcony?

INES: It's the only way out!

ALONSO: Tell me the truth:
    How high?

INES: We're on the second floor.
    What are you waiting for it's time?

ALONSO: The second floor? I'll break a leg!

To the audience.

> A thought for all true lovers.
> If escapades such as this one
> Prove troublesome for those of you
> Who woo your sweethearts in earnest,
> Spare a thought for the pain of one
> Who was only ever pretending.
> My curse upon all true lovers!

Exit ALONSO and MOSCATEL. Exit INES.

End of Act Two.

ACT THREE

SCENE ONE

The house of DON PEDRO. Enter INES and BEATRIZ.

INES:	They jumped off that balcony
	Like a pair of Lucifers, falling…
BEATRIZ:	Oh, no, Ines! What happened next?
INES:	Two men appeared out of nowhere
	Drew their swords and started a fight
	Suffice to say, master and man
	Rebuffed the attack, one used his head,
	While the other took to his heals.
BEATRIZ:	What are you saying?
INES:	What happened!
BEATRIZ:	But who told you all this, Ines?
INES:	Every word I am telling you
	Was told me by the servant of
	The gallant with the broken leg,
	That heroic man who jumped off
	The balcony to save your skin.
BEATRIZ:	Who imparted the laceration?
	Who caused the wounds?
INES:	Strangers!
BEATRIZ:	Then he reclines somewhere in pain?
INES:	With a sore head and a broken leg.
BEATRIZ:	Must he be always *claudicante*?
INES:	Claudi-who? What do you mean?
	I thought you'd given up big words!
BEATRIZ:	Was there ever a more ignorant
	Or illiterate woman!
	It may be said that a person
	Unable to ambulate
	In smooth and even fashion

66

Is *claudicante*, now, do you see?

INES: I've no idea what you're saying!
All I know is a gentleman,
Is laid up somewhere and he's hurt.

BEATRIZ: And I, oh heaven, feel his pain.
What poison has my soul imbibed
What insanity, what passion
What outrage, what torment,
Has breached the portals of my ears
Conceiving in me something
That these feelings may yet abort?
What is passing through me?
Were I able to comprehend
I could, perhaps, describe, explain.
The god of love, god of fools
Hearing me insult his power
Has cursed me and the more
I deny his deity the more
He punishes me with stirring
I fail as yet to comprehend.
A man entered my private room
With boldness and resolution
Taking responsibility for his deeds
But his generous actions leave me
With a deep sense of obligation
Though his words of love left me
With a serious sense of offence.
Strange that one might feel both
Offended and obliged together.
My father came into the room
And tragic might have been the result
Had the gallant gentleman not
Followed to the letter all the
Instructions I imparted:
For my sake, he concealed himself
For my sake, jumped from a height
For my sake he was injured by

An unknown hand, thus I remain,
With grievance and gratitude,
Not knowing which to preference.
Empathy for his suffering
Is improper yet to ignore one's
Obligations would be impolite,
I'm offended he came to woo, yet
Regret he suffered in my cause:
If one begins feeling gratitude
May one ultimately fall in love?

INES: Madam, what pain do you endure?
Why do you weep so bitterly?

BEATRIZ: Would you have me other than I am?

INES: Don't throw away the dawn's white pearls
You might be needing them anon.

BEATRIZ: Oh, Ines, my dearest, Ines.
If you could keep my secret safe
I could share my torment with you.

INES: My heart is a strong box in which
Your secrets will always be safe

BEATRIZ: Then I'll trust you with my secret.
I wish to express my gratitude
To that gallant young gentleman,
To thank him for the injuries
He has suffered on my behalf,
But I don't wish him to know
About my concern for his pain.
I wish to be compassionate,
But remain, as I must, aloof
Loyal to my obligation
Yet steadfast in my honour,
So, not for his sake, but my own,
I wish to know more of his hurt.

INES: *(Aside.)* So there we have it, finally
The lady's heart begins to melt.

BEATRIZ: I would like you to visit him,

As if the idea were your own
And then on my behalf you will
Conduct a study of his wounds.

INES: Anything else?

BEATRIZ: You will give him
A ribbon, but you must tell him
You took it without my knowledge.

INES: I will perform this delicate task
As you yourself would have it done.
Now fetch the ribbon and see how
Fast these legs will run your errand.

BEATRIZ: I shall go and fetch the token.
But promise me, dearest Ines,
Share none of this with Leonor.

INES: I'll tell her nothing, I promise.

Exit BEATRIZ. Enter LEONOR.

INES: *(To audience.)* So, love claims another victim.

LEONOR: Ines, why are you so happy?

INES: I think I'd better tell you later:
No, I'd better tell you now
Because, as God is my witness
If I don't get this out I'll burst.
Your little trick has had a big
Effect on Beatriz.

LEONOR: What effect?

INES: She trusted me with a secret.
When I'm trusted with a secret
Something inside makes me want to
Run and shout it from the roof-tops:
If it was just harmless secret
I'd tell it, if only because
I'd been promised to secrecy.
Beatriz wants Don Alonso.
He spoke such sweet words to her
That despite her best inclination
She's sending me to his house

With a ribbon: you see, the woman,
Is a woman, is a woman.
I'd better go fetch the token.
Remember, you know none of this.

LEONOR: I'll tell her nothing, I promise.

Exit LEONOR. Enter DON JUAN.

JUAN: I overheard your conversation.
How remiss I was to expect
Loyalty in a house such as this.
Oh Leonor, love it seems has
A finite quality, as it grows
With Beatriz it declines with you.

LEONOR: Does my love, decline?

JUAN: It does.
Until this moment I have borne
My misfortunes in silence,
Hoping you might confess them
Without needing to be asked,
And though I must suffer them
You won't ask me to die without
Being able to express them, though
I must die without avenging them.
At your request Don Alonso
Visited this house to feign love
For Beatriz, whether this ploy
Was good or bad is not in question,
To protect her from discomfort
Careless of the danger to himself
He threw himself from a balcony,
As I stood below, monitoring
The unfolding of these events,
And Don Alonso descended
I was witness to the arrival
Of two men, I withdrew, quickly
Lest awareness of my presence
Should add further to their alarm:

From the shelter of my doorway
I heard the clash of blade on blade
And rushed with all possible speed
To the scene, but when I arrived
The strangers had disappeared
And Don Alonso lay bleeding.
Oh, my Leonor, could there be
Any greater cause for distress,
When Don Alonso's false love
Has led me to discover sound
Reasons for true jealousy?
When a man is stabbed in the street
Merely because he emerges
From your house, is it not clear
Something is happening inside
Most injurious to my honour?
For your sake, and for my own
I chose to remain silent, til
I could learn the identity
Oh, Leonor, of the stranger,
But my efforts in that direction,
Have been in vain and to prevent
My jealous rage letting slip
Any hint of this disgrace, I came
To let my tongue resolve what
Unluckily my sword could not.
So, farewell, inconstant one
I've made my case, I'll not be moved.

LEONOR: I have a sister, who perhaps...

JUAN: No you do not: for it is clear
If you had a sister you knew
To have a lover, why would you,
Either in jest or in earnest
Attempt to incriminate her?
As you invented a false lover
One must assume that she did not
Already possess a true one!

LEONOR: In the name of heaven…

JUAN: I did not come
To listen to your excuses!

LEONOR: Don Juan, I offer no excuse:
I have never done you wrong.

JUAN: You are guilty. My love is dead.

Exit DON JUAN. Exit LEONOR.

SCENE TWO

The house of Don Alonso.

Enter ALONSO and MOSCATEL.

MOSCATEL: Master, what's wrong? Can you tell me?
What are you thinking? Or dreaming?
What's going on in your head?
You in despair? You in distress?
Has one blow had such an effect?
Has a fall from a balcony
Wounded your sense of humour?

ALONSO: Alas! Alas! I've no idea
What's going on inside me
Happy I sometimes feel then sick.
Joyful I feel sometimes then strange
It's a bliss that becomes a grief
A blessing that becomes a curse.
A strange sickness that destroys,
Even as it heals, a poison
Which is both venom and antidote.

MOSCATEL: So, we're all in the same boat!

ALONSO: Why are you laughing?

MOSCATAL: No reason!

ALONSO: Oh! Alas!

MOSCATEL: Again!

ALONSO: Again, what?
Moscatel, will you stop laughing!

MOSCATEL: Master, you sighed!

ALONSO: And what of that?

MOSCATEL: How easily do you noblemen,
Deceive yourselves, 'alas', master
Love's got you in his cruel trap!

ALONSO: Now I'm certain that you're drunk!
I love?

MOSCATEL: You love!

ALONSO: What do you see
In me, that might lead you to
Imagine something so perverse?

MOSCATEL: Things you've said, things you haven't.

ALONSO: With whom have I fallen in love?
The only woman I've been close to
In days, is Beatriz.

MOSCATEL: Is Beatriz!

ALONSO: Me, fall in love with that woman?
That Ovid in a stupid dress
That Virgil in a silly skirt
That Cicero in petticoats?

MOSCATEL: Master! Did you not tell me
She was not as ridiculous
As Don Juan reported?

ALONSO: I did.

MOSCATEL: Do you not praise her beauty?

ALONSO: I do.

MOSCATEL: Were you not furious to find
Two men under her balcony
Ready to fight in her defence?

ALONSO: I'd good reason to be angry!

MOSCATEL: Yes, because you were jealous!

ALONSO: No!
I didn't fight with those men
In jealous rage but because
They attacked me with swords:

And my visit to Beatriz
Was a game, a charade, a joke.
Performed for my friend, Don Juan
What a pathetic conclusion if
The joke turned out to be on me!

MOSCATEL: Into the plaza, one hot afternoon
Rode a brave young toreador
Chancing his arm with lance and bull
His sponsor looking proudly on.
Gracefully he flicked his golden cape
Casually doffed his sombrero
Then lowered his mighty lance
Twenty paces from the bull pen:
The bull appeared and head to head
Towards the horse he charged.
But haunch to haunch it seems they met
As from the backside of both beasts
A mighty explosion was heard
As if each had received an enema
One with a horn, one with a lance.
The young toreador was tossed
Onto the bull, his sponsor rushed
Into the ring to attack the beast
He stabbed, but missed, striking his friend.
And the young man stood up and yelled:
'Who is this man sponsoring
Me or the bull, does anybody know?'
No one could answer his question.
Don Juan was your sponsor
When you went to see Beatriz.
And you made a terrible mess,
But no one knows if Don Juan was
Sponsoring you or Beatriz.

ALONSO: Enough, that's enough, your story
Is hardly relevant to me.

MOSCATEL: Relevant or not, I thank God
You can no longer laugh at lovers

                   As you sir, have joined the dance.

ALONSO: If that's true, Moscatel, you can

                   Tell me the name of your sweetheart.

INES calls, off.

ALONSO: Go and see who's at the door.

MOSCATEL: Who's there?

INES: Moscatel, I've come

                   To see your master.

MOSCATEL: *(Aside.)*   Oh God, what's this?

                   (To INES.) Fickle woman! In heaven's name:

                   Why are you here?

INES: Why do you think?

                   (Aside.) I want him to misunderstand

                   You see there's nothing I like more

                   Than making him feel jealous.

                   (Aside to MOSCATEL) Don Alonso must know I am

                   The kind of girl who keeps her word.

                   I'm here to protect my good name.

MOSCATEL: You'll get a good name coming here.

INES: Move!

MOSCATEL: You can't come in!

INES: Away!

ALONSO: Who are you speaking to?

MOSCATEL: No one!

INES: Liar! You're speaking to someone!

ALONSO: To a most important someone!

                   Dear Ines, a thousand kisses!

INES: A thousand, thousand, if you like!

                   And then again, one more. Again.

MOSCATEL pinches INES.

INES: Ow!

ALONSO: What was that?

INES: You stabbed me:

        With the hilt of your dagger, sir.

ALONSO: Ines, you've come to restore me
    Body and soul, for though you sent
    An angry reply to my invitation,
    You know how much I love you
    And hope you won't remain aloof.

INES: I was never angry with you
    As soon as I got your message
    I sent word I'd come and visit.

ALONSO: Servant-scum, did you lie to me?

MOSCATEL: Me sir?

ALONSO: As God is my witness
    I'll kick you into an early grave!

MOSCATEL: *(Aside.)* Cuckolded: then kicked to death.
    Next I'll have to sing him a song.

INES: *(Aside.)* When he knows why I'm really here
    He'll get better soon enough.
    Let him be jealous a bit longer.

MOSCATEL: Will you take the word of a whore?

INES: You rogue address your mistress
    With a little respect if you please.
    I'd like to speak to you alone.

MOSCATEL: Alone!

ALONSO: Get outside. Guard the door.

MOSCATEL: *(Aside.)* Guard the door? Oh, God almighty!

ALONSO: What did you say?

MOSCATEL: I said, sir,
    That I am your loyal servant
    And I'll not permit this outrage.
    I will not allow this trollop
    To tempt you into activities
    Which could do damage to your health.

ALONSO: Since when have you been concerned
    For my health? Go and guard the door.

MOSCATEL: Sir, you will have to kill me first.
    I will lay down my life for yours.

ALONSO: But you've never shown this kind of
                Loyalty before.

MOSCATEL: I was saving it up:
                For a moment like this.

ALONSO: Get out!

ALONSO pushes MOSCATEL out of the door.

ALONSO: Ines, we're alone, why don't you
                Return to my arms?

INES: You think
                I'm the kind of woman who'd come
                To your house for hugs and kisses!
                I am here because I was sent
                And not because I chose to be.
                I was pretending when I came in.

ALONSO: But, I don't understand this at all.

INES: Then, I'll explain, sir, briefly:
                Having heard there was a sword fight
                Outside her front door, in which
                You were injured, my mistress,
                Feeling a certain sympathy
                For your injuries and feeling
                An obligation for your actions
                And a concern for your health,
                Sent me here to study your wounds
                And to give you this silk ribbon
                Which, she asked me to say, I stole
                But which is, in fact, a love token
                Given of her own free will. So.
                Job done, now I'm off.

ALONSO: Listen. Wait.
                Does Beatriz remember me?
                Is she concerned for my health?
                And has she sent me a token?
                This seems strange.

INES: Not to me, sir.
          Your wooing was a bogus game

So, she was bound to fall for it:
We women never get it right
And the liar always does better
Than the man who truly loves.

Enter MOSCATEL.

MOSCATEL: *(Aside.)* The jealous man suffers as much
As a man condemned to death!
I've come to see the bitter truth,
Better to see than imagine.

ALONSO: Beautiful, Ines, as Beatriz
Has sung so violently from one
Extreme to another I shall
Follow her example, and though
I didn't woo her like a gentleman
I shall proceed like one. Wait here
While I write her a letter.

MOSCATEL: *(Aside.)* He's gone, now I can breathe again.
(Aloud.) You, Hircanian, tigress!
You base, Egyptian crocodile!
You vile, poisonous serpent!
You cruel Albanian lion!
How can my mind conjure the thoughts
How can my mouth shape the words
To do justice to your crimes.

INES: They can't.

MOSCATEL: If words can't do the job, these hands
Can slap your face!

INES: No, they can't!
Stop it! That's enough! Game over.
I was taking my revenge on you
Because you doubted my purity.

MOSCATEL: Your purity! Don't make me laugh!

INES: I didn't come here…

MOSCATEL: You lied to me!

INES: To see your master…

MOSCATEL: Why did you come?

INES:	To bring him…
MOSCATEL:	What?
INES:	A ribbon!
MOSCATEL:	What…?
INES:	Which, belongs to Beatriz.
	Who is learning how to speak.
MOSCATEL:	And the kisses?
INES:	Meant nothing!
	No harm done, he grabbed by body
	You've got my soul.
MOSCATEL:	Treacherous beauty!
	If you'd give another your body
	Then let the devil take your soul.
INES:	It was a joke!
MOSCATEL:	It wasn't funny!
	A joke? Never let it be said
	Moscatel, couldn't take a joke.
	Come to my arms.
INES:	Of course I will!

Enter DON ALONSO.

ALONSO:	What's this?
INES:	It's called kissing
	Where I come from:
MOSCATEL:	Master:
	I was so happy when I heard
	The shrew was coming round:
	Forgive my curiosity, I was
	Listening to your conversation
	That I hugged Ines, to thank her
	For bringing you the ribbon.
ALONSO:	Ines, come here, take this letter
	Deliver it to your mistress,
	For your trouble, a diamond ring.
INES:	For this gift, I wish you could
	Live as long as the Phoenix bird.

Exit INES.

MOSCATEL: You gave her a diamond?

ALONSO: I did.

MOSCATEL: For nothing!

ALONSO: Don't be foolish.

MOSCATEL: Let a thousand wicked devils
Drag me off to hell if you're not
Madly in love with Beatriz.

ALONSO: Why do you keep repeating that?

MOSCATEL: Because you just gave a maid
A diamond ring for delivering
A letter to a woman from whom
You can hope to get very little
In return and that's not like you.

ALONSO: It was an act of gratitude;
I'm grateful, I am not in love.

MOSCATEL: Sir, can we settle our accounts?
I cannot remain in this house.

ALONSO: Why not, Moscatel?

MOSCATEL: Because,
I can't work for a lovesick master
Who neglects his servant, spending
All his time serving his sweetheart.

ALONSO: Is this my reward for putting up
With your nonsense?

MOSCATEL: It's over!

Enter DON JUAN.

DON JUAN: What's over!

ALONSO: He's leaving me.

JUAN: Why is that Moscatel?

MOSCATEL: Because,
He's committed the worst betrayal
The human heart can conceive:
The most wicked, treacherous act
The human mind can imagine.

JUAN: What's he done?

MOSCATEL: He's fallen in love.
So, I've good reason to leave him.

ALONSO: He's spouting this nonsense
Because he's seen with what courtesy
I treat Beatriz, for the sake
Of your love.

JUAN: We must thank love...

ALONSO: For what?

JUAN: For freeing you
From any further obligation.
Today my love expired.

ALONSO: But what of
Leonor?

JUAN: Is dead to my heart.
Love is a close ally of fortune
So is subject to constant change.
How is your love, Don Alonso?

ALONSO: I shall never speak to her, no
Nor look upon her face again.
Why should a man who has endured
Such injuries return to her street
To talk to her, or gaze on her,
When he whose head is untouched
Will not.

JUAN: I can never go back.
For the injuries I endure
Are the cruel wounds of jealousy
Such injuries are most hurtful
For they strike the immortal soul.

ALONSO: I'd willingly swap wounds with you!
For whether slight or serious
I'd much prefer a bruised soul
To lacerated skull. It is clear:
When a cut is badly treated one dies.
Even the most homespun remedies

	Can cure jealousy.
JUAN:	Don Alonso, I will never again ask you To place yourself in such A difficult situation.
ALONSO:	But don't give up on my behalf. These scrapes are nothing to me.
JUAN:	For your sake and for my own I retire, you have endured enough.
ALONSO:	A battle-hardened war horse, like Myself can carry an injury.
JUAN:	Don Alonso, forgive me, I'll never return to that house!
ALONSO:	If I'm not to return for your sake I must return to discover The name of my assailant.
JUAN:	If there is a matter of honour Steps can be taken, privately.
ALONSO:	I've always been more concerned To maintain my reputation Among women than amongst men So, it would be wrong to allow A woman as proud as Beatriz...
JUAN:	My friend, I will find a way to Disabuse her.
ALONSO:	Don Juan, Don Juan Let me make this crystal clear: I mean to visit Beatriz!
MOSCATEL:	*(Aside.)* And finally the truth comes out. Sometimes my boss is such a liar.
JUAN:	If it's that important to you You must return, I wish you luck.
ALONSO:	You know I can't visit her unless You and Leonor cover my back.
JUAN:	I shall never speak to her again.
ALONSO:	For my sake, Don Juan, you must.

	After all, it is not unusual
	In Madrid, for a gentleman
	To speak with a former lover
	In order to help out a friend.
JUAN:	For your sake, I will undertake
	A thing I swore I never would.
MOSCATEL:	*(Aside.)* Why do these noblemen go all
	Around the houses sounding off
	When they both quite obviously
	Want to go and see the ladies.
JUAN:	For your sake, I will return,
	But remember there will be
	Cupboards!
ALONSO:	Which won't be a problem.
JUAN:	And a balcony!
ALONSO:	Which is not an issue.
JUAN:	And swords!
ALONSO:	There'll be no more sword play!
	Love created a deal of strife
	In response to a simple hoax
	But now I go with honest intent
	Let cupboards, balconies and swords
	Do their worst, I defy them all!

SCENE THREE

A street in Madrid. Enter DON DIEGO and DON LUIS.

DIEGO:	You know the spirit in which
	I serve you.
LUIS:	I do and I
	Value our friendship, Don Diego,
	You have always supported me
	With sound advice and good judgement.
DIEGO:	Then you will not take it amiss,
	If I offer a slight rebuke?
LUIS:	No!

DEIGO: Don Luis, the events of last night...

LUIS: If you are about to tell me
It was an act of madness, I agree!
To strike a gentleman in the street
Who had offered me no challenge
My excuse is that I have none.
I shall take steps to remedy
The situation, for the man who
Lets the madness of jealousy
Cloud his judgement, may also
Allow himself to be led astray
In matters of greater importance.

DIEGO: How do you intend to manage
The project already in motion?
Don Pedro is surely aware
Of your intentions.

LUIS: Not a problem.
Marriages have been annulled
After sacred vows have been sworn
Why should I fear to change my plans
This affair has never been to church.

Enter DON PEDRO.

PEDRO: *(Aside.)* Suspicion hangs over my house
I have ice burning in my heart
And a fire freezing in my gut
Which is why I wander the streets
At this late hour looking to find
Don Luis and settle this matter:
Better to end all doubt now than
Allow the actions of that most
Notorious young man to bring
More shame upon my house.
And here is Don Luis, looking
So smart, so well bred, he's the one.

DIEGO: You father-in-law approaches.

LUIS: My father-in-law? Let's go!

PEDRO: Don Luis, I've been informed by
Relatives of yours, that you intend
To bring honour to my house,
I have sought you out so I might
Express my gratitude and tell you
How proud it would make me…

LUIS: Don Pedro, sir, I am a man
For whom the joy of yesterday
Has become the sadness of today.
I had, indeed, dared to aspire
In the direction you indicate
And am pleased my aspirations
Are greeted with such joy but in
The midst of all this good fortune
I have encountered misfortune:
I must bring to your attention
A serious matter of honour
Which has arisen and which I fear
Must cast doubt upon our plans.

PEDRO: *(Aside.)* A serious matter of honour?
Help, heaven!
(Aloud.)   Must cast doubt?

LUIS: Indeed!

PEDRO: *(Aloud.)* But, what? *(Aside.)* I will surely expire.
(Aloud.) How has Beatriz offended?

LUIS: Sir, do not misunderstand me.
Your passion leads you astray:
The matter of honour to which
I refer is no…

PEDRO: What is the matter?

LUIS: Having learnt that His Majesty
Whom the heavens defend,
He is the star of our sphere,
He is the planet of our land
Intends to set forth this spring
To fight a holy war: discovering

He had invited a noble gentleman,
Who happily is a relative of mine
To muster a troop, I begged him
To entrust me with a company,
He has honoured my request.
And it is this enterprise which
Denies me the opportunity
Of marrying your daughter,
For he who tries to be both
Husband and soldier is often
Neither soldier nor husband.
Should I return safely to Madrid
We can perhaps return to our plans
But as you see, at this moment
Contracting marriage to Beatriz
Is in conflict with my honour.

Exit DON DIEGO and DON LUIS.

PEDRO: 'Is in conflict with my honour'.
Oh, lord, carry me up to heaven,
What have I seen? What have I heard?
I am troubled! I am stunned!
I can hardly catch my breath!
It is foolish of me to torment
Myself like this, if the matter
Of honour is as he describes:
I must beware, the wretched mind
Thinks only wretched thoughts.

Exit DON PEDRO.

SCENE FOUR

The house of Don Pedro. Enter BEATRIZ and INES.

BEATRIZ: Why did he give you this letter?

INES: He is a very generous man.

BEATRIZ: Perhaps you told him I sent you?

INES: You've no reason to distrust me.

	I didn't say you'd sent the ribbon
	And I didn't say you'd sent me.
	I respect you, you're my mistress:
	You've trusted me with your secret.
BEATRIZ:	If what you say is true, then why
	Would he have the slightest reason
	To give you a letter?
INES:	*(Aside.)* She thinks
	She's got me there, but no chance.
	(Aloud.) He asked me to take the letter
	And pass it to you, if I could.
	I took it, so he'd think I was on his side.
	I reckon he thought if I was
	Capable of stealing a ribbon
	And getting it to him, I might be able
	To get you to accept his letter.
BEATRIZ:	I am satisfied with your reply
INES:	And I'm glad to be of service.
	Be careful, here comes Leonor!
BEATRIZ:	She mustn't see me with this letter.

BEATRIZ hides the letter. Enter LEONOR.

LEONOR:	Now I could say and with good cause:
	What clandestine communiqué
	Do you crumple and secrete?
BEATRIZ:	And I could say, with equal cause:
	Since you're not prepared to listen
	To that which I am keen to share
	Why would I ever show you this?

Exit BEATRIZ.

LEONOR:	Ines!
INES:	I'll die if I don't get this out!
LEONOR:	Quick! Tell me about the letter!
INES:	You don't understand me do you?
	Do you have to spoil everything?
	Why couldn't you wait to be told?

I get pangs of conscience if I don't
Reveal a secret before I'm asked.

Enter BEATRIZ, concealed.

BEATRIZ: I know it's wrong to listen like this,
But, I'm sure they're up to something.

INES: I went to his house and the first thing
I did was tell him she'd sent me.

LEONOR: You're a genius!

BEATRIZ: *(Aside.)* And I'm a fool!
To trust my secrets to a servant.
Leonor, be careful how you tread.

INES: And then I gave him the ribbon
Of course, I told him she'd sent it.

BEATRIZ: *(Aside.)* Oh, no! Oh no! What have I done?

LEONOR: What was that? I heard something?

INES: It's Don Juan coming up the stairs.

LEONOR: But he just left in a jealous rage
Swearing never to see me again.

INES: Sometimes, madam you're so naive:
Don't you know that when a man
Is all puffed up and bellowing
'Treacherous beauty, be gone'
He's probably asking for a hug.

BEATRIZ: *(Aside.)* The story of my shame unfolds:
I'll listen to the bitter end.

Enter DON JUAN, MOSCATEL and DON ALONSO.

DON JUAN: Doubtless, Leonor, you believe
That jealousy has brought me here
To speak with you, as jealousy,
To employ common parlance
Often acts as love's go-between
Running messages back and forth:
But no, I've not returned to listen
To your excuses, for love, Leonor
Is wounded by all talk of wounds:

It is for a different purpose
I cross this threshold once again:
Grievance will always find a way.
My dear friend, Don Alonso,
Who at your request played the role
Of bogus lover to Beatriz, and
Who was expelled from this house
In a state of some indignity:
Is concerned that Beatriz might
In her vanity be harbouring
False assumptions about the true
Nature of his feelings for her
And has asked me to bring him here,
So, he might make his position clear
And relieve Beatriz of any doubt.
How could I refuse to do for him
That which he so very selflessly
Did not refuse to do for me?

BEATRIZ: *(Aside.)* What a deal of obligation.
I owe these noble gentlemen.

JUAN: That is Don Alonso's purpose.
And lest it be thought, suspected
Or imagined, that unhappiness,
Pain, or misery has provoked
My return, I'll remain outside
While Don Alonso speaks his mind
And clears any doubt, or scruple,
Or any scruple of a doubt that
May have unjustly attached itself
To his good name: Don Alonso,
As the sun descends in anguish
Into shadow, to be embraced like
A cold corpse in the arms of night,
Come forth, but beware the eternal
Vigilance of Don Pedro.

LEONOR: Don't leave, Don Juan. Wait. Don Juan.

JUAN: Wait, Leonor? Why should I wait?

LEONOR: So, I might explain...

JUAN: There's no point!

LEONOR: So, I might apologise.

JUAN: In vain!

Exit DON JUAN.

LEONOR: Do forgive me, Don Alonso,
I must follow him. I'll return.
He's jealous. I must set him straight.

Exit LEONOR.

ALONSO: Does this mean I have to leave here
Without speaking to Beatriz?

MOSCATEL: Or you might have said: 'Oh, no
We're in the same mess as last time!'

ALONSO: Ines, take me to Beatriz
I must speak to her.

BEATRIZ: Here is Beatriz,
Listening to the iniquities
Of a vile sister, a false friend
A despicable manservant,
A treacherous chambermaid
And a most pernicious lover:
In consequence of the deeds
Of Leonor and Don Juan,
Of Ines and Moscatel,
I have found if not consolation
For my woes then perhaps some
Comprehension of my folly.
Though I might easily complain
Of the unkind and hurtful, of the
Many cruel and spiteful deeds
I've experienced at your hands
Joined all together as you were
In conspiracy against me,
I have come to understand that
In the kingdom of the soul

Contempt reigns in perfect peace,
And love can have no dominion.
There is one matter, one subject
Of which I must speak, though in
Complaining I'll be offended but
Of this offence I must complain
It being the greatest of my insults
And not the least of my injuries:
For as a woman it has been
Most painful for me to discover
That a lie may more easily
Win our hearts, than the truth we love.
Sir, is my family and my blood
Of so little worth? Am I myself,
I must say this, am I myself
Of so little worth, that should a man
Presume to woo, he could only
Woo me with lies?

ALONSO: Beautiful Beatriz,
As you emerge with such dignity
From these wrongs, so deeply felt,
It will be simple to disabuse you.

BEATRIZ: How can you simply disabuse
When the abuse, sir, was complete?

ALONSO: If you listen, I will explain:
Sometimes, like a fool, a man may
Dive into the sea, imagining
Before him an orchard of foam
A forest of snow paying no heed
To the danger and in a trice,
To his horror, orchard and forest
Devour him and love is a sea
And as only a fool plays with the sea
Only a fool makes a fool of love.
As a joke or an experiment
An ingenious firework-maker
May construct a thunderbolt only

To be burnt by the heat of his
Own creation, love is a thunderbolt
And as only a fool plays with fire
Only a fool makes a fool of love.
A skilful swordsman may unsheathe
A blade playfully exchanging
Blows with his dearest friend
Only to wound him as if he were his
Keenest enemy, love is a sword
As only a fool plays with naked steel
Only a fool makes a fool of love.
In jocund mood a man may stroke
A wild creature that seems tame
Only to be savaged when the animal
Turns on him and love is a beast
And as only a fool plays with nature
Only a fool makes a fool of love.
Like a fool I jumped into the sea
Like a fool I started up a fire
Played with naked steel and beast
And I was drowned in the sea
Was scorched by a thunder bolt
Felt the violence of beast and blade
So then, if beast, blade, fire and sea
Have the power to destroy a man:
Only a fool makes a fool of love.

BEATRIZ: To that, I might reply…

Enter INES and LEONOR, running.

LEONOR: Oh, my god!
Don Juan rushed out into the street
As I called, I saw father coming
We must hide...

BEATRIZ: Too late, Leonor!

LEONOR: Don Alonso!

BEATRIZ: Today, father
Will learn what you've been doing

	I will reveal your dirty tricks.
LEONOR:	If you try to do that, Beatriz
	I'll find a way to excuse myself
	And heap all the blame on to you.
	We are both in the same mess
	Can't we resolve this together?
BEATRIZ:	If only to set you a good
	Example, I agree, to be honest:
	I'm not left with a lot of choice.
MOSCATEL:	The cupboard! The china cupboard!
	I beg the sanctuary of china.
ALONSO:	No, never, I'd prefer to take...
INES:	He is in the hall!
BEATRIZ:	Hide in here!
	Let this room be your sanctuary.
MOSCATEL:	And me, let it keep me safe as well.
ALONSO:	*(Aside.)* Is hiding a prerequisite
	For a lover? I'm not happy!
MOSCATEL:	When we're safe inside, Ines
	Go downstairs and tell the world
	Then men can attack us with swords.

DON ALONSO and MOSCATEL hide. Enter DON PEDRO.

PEDRO:	It's dark in here, bring light: Ines!
	Why must I always call for a lamp?
INES:	Here we are sir, your favourite lamp.
PEDRO:	*(Aside.)* Dishonour heaped upon my house.
	Insults thrown at me in the street.
	Merciful father in heaven
	Give me patience or give me death.
BEATRIZ:	You seem disturbed?
LEONOR:	What troubles you?
PEDRO:	I am disturbed in a question
	Of honour, troubled by insults
	Thrown at me in the street, though
	It might be more accurate to say

	Insults which thrive and multiply
	Within the walls of my own house!
LEONOR:	*(Aside.)* Oh, my god!
INES:	*(Aside.)* He knows everything!
BEATRIZ:	Dear father, can you not reveal
	The origin of your distress?
PEDRO:	Folly, Beatriz, your folly
	Is the origin of my distress!
	As a result of your foolish ways
	An arrogant young man has had
	The effrontery to impeach
	The honour of this noble house.
LEONOR:	*(Aside.)* He seems to know all our secrets.
BEATRIZ:	I sir?

MOSCATEL from the other room.

MOSCATEL:	*(Aside.)* This isn't going well!
PEDRO:	Yes, Beatriz, because of you,
	Don Luis has insulted my person
	And my house.
BEATRIZ:	*(Aside.)* What a relief!
LEONOR:	*(Aside.)* That's better, I can breathe again.

Enter DON JUAN.

JUAN:	*(Aside.)* To make a mistake once is human
	To make it twice is unforgivable:
	This time I shan't wait for the doors
	To be locked and for Don Alonso
	To descend from the balcony,
	This time, I'll make the first move!
	(Aloud.) Sir, in the name of my noble
	Family, long since tied to yours
	With bonds of love, bonds of blood...
LEONOR:	*(Aside to BEATRIZ)* What's he doing?
BEATRIZ:	*(Aside to LEONOR)* We're about to find out.
JUAN:	Bonds that I believe oblige you
	To assist me in times of peril.

             I must inform you, I have been
             Gravely insulted by three men,
             In the street outside your house:
             I'm reluctant to challenge them
             Single-handed; I feel confident
             In seeking your support in this
             For well I know the mighty Etna
             That rumbles deep inside your chest
             Though now its peaks are capped with snow.

PEDRO: Don Juan, you need say no more
             I understand the laws of honour
             And the obligations of blood
             Let's go.

JUAN: You're a man of honour,
             Don Pedro, my second father!
             (Aside to LEONOR.) As soon as I've got the old man out
             Will you get rid of Don Alonso?

DON ALONSO speaking from his hiding place.

ALONSO: *(Aside.)* These men must be my assailants.
             It's impossible to leave this room
             But it's impossible to remain.

PEDRO: I have a lucky shield: something
             I wore when I was a young man.
             I think I saw it in that room.

JUAN: Retrieve it sir, but quickly!

DON PEDRO goes into the room where DON ALONSO and MOSCATEL are hiding.

BEATRIZ: *(Aside.)* Oh, Don Alonso's sanctuary May yet
             prove to be his grave.

PEDRO: *(Off.)* Who is this, hiding!

ALONSO: *(Off.)*   A man!

MOSCATEL: *(Off.)* That's right! He's a man, I'm nothing!
             Just ignore me, I don't matter.

Enter DON ALONSO, MOSCATEL and DON PEDRO.

PEDRO: Don Juan, as I was about to

	Help you confront your enemies
	I believe that you are obliged
	To assist me in this matter
	Which is of greater consequence.
	This man has offended my honour
	It is clear, I must end his days.
ALONSO:	Don Juan, I need not remind you
	Of the obligation you owe me.
	I fight to defend my own life
	And the life of these young ladies.

DON ALONSO and PEDRO with drawn swords, DON JUAN stands between them.

LEONOR:	Oh, my god!
BEATRIZ:	What an awful mess!
JUAN:	*(Aside.)* An impossible dilemma!
PEDRO:	Do you hold back?
ALONSO:	Do not delay!
PEDRO:	I will resolve this matter without
	Your help!

DON PEDRO and DON ALONSO fight, DON JUAN trying to interject between them.

JUAN:	Don Alonso, stop!
	Good sir, cease!
PEDRO:	Do you play
	Peacemaker?
ALONSO:	Can you be so disloyal?

Voices are heard off stage.

LUIS:	*(Off.)* What's this? I hear a clash of swords
	In the house of Don Pedro!
DIEGO:	*(Off.)* Let's not delay! Let's go inside!

Enter DON LUIS and DON DIEGO.

LUIS:	Cease!
PEDRO:	What's this?
ALONSO:	Gentlemen! Beware!

LUIS: What is this?

PEDRO: This is Don Pedro!
             Taking steps to cleanse the stain
             To which you recently made reference:
             If honour forbids you marrying
             Beatriz, it bids me to take revenge.

DON LUIS: Now you know I had good reason
             To withdraw, there was an incident
             In the street, beneath your balcony...

ALONSO: This is the man who wounded me!

LUIS: Indeed!

ALONSO: Sir, I must have revenge!

JUAN: And I thank heaven my jealous
             Folly has been revealed, Leonor,
             Live once more within my heart.

To DON PEDRO.

             Sir, I must protect this woman
             Against your rage!

PEDRO: Don Juan! Don Juan!
             The only man who may presume
             To defend my daughter is the man
             Who intends to make her his wife.

ALONSO: Sir, I take you at your word.

JUAN: If the remedy is so simple
             I pledge myself to Leonor.

ALONSO: I pledge myself to Beatriz.

PEDRO: *(Aside.)* And it's best if I say nothing.
             For once the damage is done
             There's little one can do to mend it.

MOSCATEL: *(Aside.)* In the end, the wild young man
             Emerges from the game of love
             With a head wound, a limp
             And the worst of all possible
             Disasters, saddled with a wife.

INES: *(Aside.)* In the end, the most arrogant

Vain and ridiculous woman
Emerges from the game of love
Despite herself in love,
And what must be the worst of all
Disasters, married to a man.

MOSCATEL: Ines, give me your hand. Don't think.
Say yes. No more games. Love wins.

ALONSO: Wise spectators, forgive our poet
Who prostrates himself at your feet.

The End.

WWW.OBERONBOOKS.COM